Biblical
Authority

Biblical Authority

The Critical Issue for the Body of Christ

James T. Draper, Jr. & Kenneth Keathley

B&H
PUBLISHING GROUP
NASHVILLE, TENNESSEE

© 2001
by James T. Draper, Jr.

978-0-8054-2453-9

Published by B&H Publishing Group
Nashville, Tennessee

Dewey Decimal Classification: 220
Subject Heading: BIBLE

Unless otherwise noted, Scripture quotations are taken from the
Holman Christian Standard Bible, © Copyright 2000 by Holman
Bible Publishers. Used by permission. Quotations marked NASB are
from the New American Standard Bible, © the Lockman Foundation,
1960, 1962, 1963, 1968, 1971, 1972, 1973, 1975, 1977, 1995.
Used by permission.

Library of Congress Cataloging-in-Publication Data

Draper, James T.
    Biblical authority : the critical issue for the body of Christ / James T.
Draper, Jr. and Kenneth Keathley.—Rev. and updated.
    p. cm.
    Rev. ed. Of: Authority. 1984.
    Includes bibliographical references.
    ISBN 0-8054-2453-9
    Bible—Evidences, authority, etc. 2. Southern Baptist Convention—
Doctrines. 3. Baptists—Doctrines. I. Keathley, Kenneth, 1958– II.
Draper, James T. Authority. III. Title
BS480 .D72 2001
220.1'3—dc21

                                                    2001025155

Contents

Foreword

WE IN THE CHURCH TODAY face a crisis of authority. We acknowledge Jesus Christ as Lord of the church, but we ask: How does He exercise His authority in the earth today? As Christians, what is our rule of faith and order? This issue confronts virtually every communion and denomination within the body of Christ and is a chief concern of the people and churches making up the Southern Baptist Convention.

Southern Baptists are conservative theologically. We have always sought our authority in the Bible and have justly deserved to be called "people of the Book." But due to human frailty, we do not all interpret the Bible alike. Some are more conservative than others. Some take more liberties than do others. Both these camps—sometimes called "moderates" and "fundamentalists," or "liberals" and "conservatives"—have become more visible in recent years in the debate over authority.

James Draper, claiming friendship with people on both sides of the present difference in doctrine, avowed when he became president of the convention, that he *belonged* to neither side. No man has worked harder than he to bridge this difference. Drawing upon his widespread friendships, he has brought together people prominently identified with each side—if not to full agreement—at least to talk with one another.

"Jimmy," as he is affectionately called, has written this volume to set forth some basic steps toward solving the current differences. While specific in his pronouncements, he allows for those differences which are inherent in our Baptist polity and practice.

As Mission Control periodically corrects the course of NASA space vehicles, to direct them toward a destination, so Draper is calling on us to withstand the forces that would draw us off our God-appointed path. This book follows in the tradition of The Baptist Faith and Message. It is the much-needed corrective to keep Southern Baptists on target in evangelism and missions worldwide. Herein, Dr. Draper has charted a course which all of us can follow. Let us read and ponder the message, the *plea* of this book. Then, in the spirit of the author, let us unite hearts and hands as we move toward the goal dear to all our hearts—reaching the world with the saving gospel of the Lord Jesus Christ.

Herschel H. Hobbs
Late President, Southern Baptist Convention
Late Pastor, First Baptist Church
Oklahoma City, Oklahoma

Preface

THESE PAGES ARE WRITTEN out of a deep concern for the body of Christ and represent our attempt to cast some understanding on a controversy that revolves around the issue of authority.

These pages are written in love and with a keen understanding that only as we approach one another in love can we resolve critical issues such as the one before us. It is important to note that we cannot demand absolute conformity among ourselves in order for us to work and worship together. If we are God's people—saved through faith in our Lord Jesus Christ—then we have a foundation and a basis for serving God and one another. Read this in its entirety before making a final judgment on its value and propositions.

The key issue among all Christian people today is the matter of *authority*. Where does genuine authority come from? Who or what is the source of our authority? Is there a standard, a "rule" which will be authoritative for God's people today? Daily the church faces ongoing issues that demand answers. Inevitably, the answers or lack of answers relate to authority. It has become the critical issue of our times.

There are some in the church who appeal to their denominational heritage as their authority. Others rely upon the authority of educational achievement or their intellectual powers. Still others claim the authority based on the practice of our churches and conventions. If enough of us are doing it or claiming it, they say, then it must be correct. And there are many other potential sources for authority in our lives.

Although proposed sources of authority may have legitimacy in various areas of life, underlying all of them must be the one unchanging yet dynamically relevant authority, namely, the Word of God. The Scriptures must be the final ground for guidance in all arenas of life. This raises other issues. Is the Bible truth without error, or is it a book that only contains truth? Since man was uniquely involved in its delivery, is it woven both within and without with error and imperfections?

This book will examine the key issues facing us as they relate to the Word of God. We will explore the whole area of how we know what we know, how we perceive truth, and how we determine that a document such as the Bible is truth without error.

Next, we will consider the three possible foundations for ultimate human authority. These, as we shall see, are rationalism or reason, ecclesiastical fiat, and divine revelation in the Bible. To understand how we have arrived at this crucial point in the controversy over authority, we will look at four rather modern developments and see how they affect modern theological thought:

1. The historical-critical approach to Scripture,
2. The rise of existential philosophy,
3. The impact of naturalistic and uniformitarian science, and
4. The presumed contributions of major world religions.

As we consider these we will observe the manner in which many in the church have shifted from divine revelation to rationalism as their ultimate base of authority. This tragic shift has led us into religious experience without theological foundation, situational ethics without absolutes, and evangelism without an adequate biblical concept of our lost condition or God's revealed response.

An essential part in determining the critical issue facing the body of Christ today will be a review of what church leaders through the centuries have believed with regard to authority. Since we are Southern Baptists, we will also look at the developing history of the Southern Baptist Convention to discover what the early founders and leaders believed about the authority of Scripture. It is very important for us to know our heritage. Without that, the issue today would be meaningless.

We will see what the Bible says about itself, and we will study the meaning of biblical inspiration. This book is *not* about inerrancy or inspiration. It is about authority. Inerrancy and inspiration are related topics, but they are not the critical issue. There is also a chapter included dealing with the sufficiency of Scripture, which is vital to this entire subject. The Scripture is absolutely sufficient for every challenge of our modern world today.

Finally, we will address ourselves to the future. Where do we go from here? With the proper base of authority, what should we become in this twenty-first century? It is not necessary that we be conformed absolutely to one viewpoint, but there must be limits beyond which we cannot go. We will endeavor to suggest the direction that must be taken if we are to remain a vital, aggressive part of the Lord's work in this world.

This book is a labor of love. We are committed to serving our Lord through every opportunity He provides, and we ask that these pages be received in the context of our love and our commitment to God and His Word. With hearts full of joy, excitement, and anticipation, we look at the unprecedented opportunities before us and the absolute necessity for the proper authority required to meet these unfolding challenges.

James T. Draper, Jr.
Kenneth D. Keathley

A Tragic Step That Can Lead to Spiritual Disaster

"There are people among us today, teaching in our academic institutions, laboring in our denominations, pastoring in our churches, who have not departed all that far from classic biblical doctrine. They still believe that Jesus is God. They still believe in the bodily resurrection of Christ. They still believe in the virgin birth. But they do not believe that everything in Scripture is necessarily accurate and without error. They have started over the edge."

THE CHRISTIAN COMMUNITY in recent years has taken a tragic step in its theological commitment. Sometimes consciously, sometimes subconsciously, but always tragically, many professing Christians have slowly moved away from the historic position on the nature of the Bible. Little or large, deliberate or not, when one takes such a step he courts disaster in his life and ministry. When one takes that tragic step the result is usually a loss of mission and evangelistic zeal; theological defection; undue emphasis upon the material and temporal with a corresponding loss of consciousness of the eternal; reliance upon mystical, personal experience instead of revealed truth; unjustified

attachment to human reasoning—to name but a few spiritually destructive results.

The basic problem that we face today has to do with knowledge and truth. It is not the *quantity* of truth which is being debated, but the *source* of truth. Where does genuine truth originate, and how can we know that something is actually truth? This is the burning issue challenging every serious Bible student and Christian today. Philosophically, we refer to this whole area of study as *epistemology*. Epistemology deals with how we know what we know and how we know what is true. The word *epistemology* comes from the Greek verb *epistomai,* which means "to know" or "to understand." This is very basic to the entire discussion concerning the problem in modern theology because it brings us to the question of ultimate authority. How can we analyze the competing claims to truth? There are three basic possibilities. These are (1) human reason, (2) ecclesiastical authority, and (3) divine revelation.

The person holding to human reason (or rationalism) believes he is his own final authority. The question then is which method that individual will use in testing truth claims. The options available to him can be grouped under three headings: *rationalism, empiricism,* and *mysticism.* The rationalist believes he or she can determine what is true by reason alone, because of innate or natural abilities within the human mind. The empiricist places confidence in experimentation and in the observation of sense phenomena, affirming as true only that which can be physically demonstrated. Finally, there is the mystic, who rejects rationalism and empiricism because he recognizes that the individual is not capable of arriving at ultimate truth either by reason or observation. The mystic, however, believes that the individual does possess irrational abilities that enable him to intuit truth. Truth, the mystic contends,

cannot be known objectively; it can be encountered only subjectively. No matter which of the three approaches are employed by human reason, they all have this in common: They make the individual the final arbiter of truth.

Rationalism and empiricism have much more in common with each other than with mysticism, and for our purposes, these two fall basically under the same category. This is because whether we believe that ultimate truth is a product of what goes on in our minds instinctively or whether it is something put into our minds by what we see, experience, or experiment with, all of it still comes down to a matter of one's own personal mind, reason, and experience as being the ultimate determination of truth.

Some people may be surprised that we also place mysticism under the category of rationalism. But the concept that truth, or at least insight, pops into our minds through some mystical experience—which we can then use to analyze and evaluate phenomena—is still a human-centered approach to truth. Taken together, all of these still make the human mind the ultimate authority, whether it be by intrinsic ability, mystical infiltration, or experimentation and sense experience. All of these processes bring the human mind ultimately to the forefront as the final source of authority.

Whatever is to be evaluated as true or false must pass through the filter of my own mind, my own intelligence. Whether it be instinctively perceived, informed by experimentation and observation, or informed by some presumed mystical experience, it is, nonetheless, what I think that ultimately determines what is true. This essentially represents rationalism.

The second basic possibility for determining what is true is ecclesiastical authority. This is not quite so confusing and is easier to handle. This approach, in effect, says that my church is ultimate authority. Regardless of whether I think something is right or not, if the church says it is right, then it is right for me. Regardless of any other aspect of authority, the church is my ultimate authority.

The classic example, of course, would be the Roman Catholic Church. The faithful Roman Catholic is supposed to receive the dogma of the church as being of God, as being absolute and final truth. Even Scripture is subservient to ecclesiastical authority, because, according to the Roman Church, the Bible is the product of the church. Mother church produced even the Scriptures, and, although they claim that Scripture does not contradict the dogma of the church, nonetheless, even if it did, church authority would prevail because the church is the mother of Scripture. So, ultimately and finally, what is right and wrong, what is true and false is determined by what the church officially has determined through its pronouncements.

The third possible basis of authority is divine revelation. This actually falls into two areas—general or natural revelation, which is the revelation of God in His creation, and special revelation, which is the Word of God. Today this means Scripture, since the biblical writers are no longer on the scene. We do not believe that Scripture is still being written today.

The position espoused above—that special revelation is found only in the Bible—is being challenged today by those influenced by the charismatic movement. They contend that God privately reveals Himself and His will to certain individuals. Often they will speak of receiving a "word of knowledge" that comes directly from God to the believer. The question of private revelation and the impact that this view has on the authority of Scripture will be examined more thoroughly in chapter 6.

Here, then, we have the three possible bases of ultimate authority. Although most people do not stop to consider it, everyone operates from one of these bases. For example, Martin Luther said, "My conscience is captive to the Word of God." That means that when I think one thing but the Bible says something else, then the Bible is true and my thinking is false, and I must adjust my thinking to what the Bible declares. Luther was operating from the base of divine revelation.

Any time a person says, "I do not believe the Bible is correct at this point," he or she is operating from the base of rationalism or human reason. The very fact that one regards the Bible as incorrect indicates in itself that one has some authority that transcends the Bible. We cannot correct something unless we have something that is more accurate, more nearly true, more authoritative than the thing which we are correcting. So, any time a person finds any supposed flaw or untruth in Scripture, something which would tend to militate against its accuracy, he or she has demonstrated by that statement that he or she has a higher basis of authority than Scripture. Presumably, this could be either ecclesiastical authority or rationalism, but in virtually every instance the source of authority will be rationalism.

This is the prevailing base of authority in our day as a result of modern science, of philosophical presuppositions, and of some of the comparative studies in religion. We have now come to the point where we feel that our own reason and our own experience must be the final criterion by which all is to be judged. The mind of modern man has become all important.

After filtering the Bible through the grid of his mind, William Newton Clarke drew an intellectual conclusion with reference to the New Testament writers' expectations of the imminent return of Jesus Christ. "I perceived that writers in the Bible had recorded unquestioning expectation of the almost immediate occurrence of an event that has never occurred at all. Certainly they were in error on that point. Their inspiration, of whatever kind it was, was not a safeguard against this error, but allowed them, or rather impelled them, to work their mistaken view of the immediate future into our holy book. . . . I was not required to accept all statements in the Bible as true and all views that it contained as correct."[1] This is a classic example of the working of rationalism in its attitude toward Scripture.

Historically, biblical Christianity has been based upon divine revelation, but today that position is being severely challenged. There was a time when the faithful, who were biblical theists, did not question the conviction that the ultimate authority was Scripture. Whether they understood it or not, whether they agreed with it or not, whether they were able to penetrate into its meaning totally or not, it was nonetheless their final authority. However, for reasons that we will discuss in later chapters, that is now breaking down very remarkably and very quickly. We are seeing people who call themselves evangelicals operating from a different base of authority.

This is crucial. Even though people may deviate only slightly from the orthodox doctrines of the faith, if they have shifted to another base of authority they have nonetheless taken a very tragic step which may then lead them into further error. Even if they do not go on to further rejection of Scripture, they have opened the door for that possibility. Tragically, those to whom they minister or those whom they teach are likely to take these concepts to their logical conclusion.

At Six Flags Over Texas there used to be a great slide coming off the giant oil derrick. I can still recall the first time I went up on that thing with my children, who were quite young at the time. They were not allowed to go down by themselves because they were too small, but they could go down with an adult. I happened to be the adult. Sitting down on a burlap bag, with one child in front of me between my legs, I pushed myself over the edge and started down this frightening slope. As I did, I was tempted to reach out and grab the side. I found myself saying, *I don't really want to go down there this way. I am not sure just exactly how it will be when I go down there. I am not sure but that I might turn over or lose my grip on my son. . . .* All kinds of terrible things went through my mind and imagination.

Many who have abandoned divine revelation as their final basis of authority have looked down at where they were going and, not liking what they saw, have reached out and grabbed the side; they are just hanging on. There is no logical reason why they should not just go on down. But they simply do not want to go down. So there they hang, still fairly close to the top but in a very unstable position.

There are people among us today, teaching in our academic institutions, laboring in our denominations, pastoring in our churches, who have not departed all that far from classic biblical doctrine. They still believe that Jesus is God. They still believe in the bodily resurrection of Christ. They still believe in the virgin birth. But they do not believe that everything in Scripture is necessarily accurate and without error. They have started over the edge. They have abandoned divine revelation as their final basis of authority, however slight that deviation may seem to them.

They do not want to slide all the way down to liberalism. They do not want to deny the faith outright. They do not want to reject all the basic doctrines of Christianity. They have simply grabbed hold of the side and stayed somewhere near the top. They profess most of the doctrines, but they claim there are some errors in the Bible.

This stance may be almost imperceptible. There may not be a deliberate abandonment of a doctrinal position. They may not even know that they have headed downhill. But they are in an unstable position. Whether such individuals ever let go and slip further down or not, they are still in an unstable position. They are at least admitting the possibility of going further. It is also likely that those to whom they minister or those whom they teach will go a lot farther down than they do.

The unintended consequence of a downhill slide is illustrated abundantly in church history. In recent times, many people who advocate women as pastors are nonetheless strongly opposed to recognition of homosexual unions. Yet the arguments used by evangelical feminists to justify female pastors are in turn used by some activists to rationalize gay and lesbian marriages. Proponents of women in the pastorate generally react strongly when this is pointed out to them, but it does not make it any less true. If the silence of the four Gospels concerning women in positions of spiritual leadership can be used to overturn the clear injunctions of the apostle Paul that forbid women exercising spiritual authority over men, then the very same tack can be taken (and has been taken) with the issue of homosexuality.

Every generation of students tends to take the teachings of its professors further than the professors themselves. If there is an opening, if there is a loophole, if there is some place to go with the teaching, they will go. Once we depart from divine revelation, we have at least opened the door to whatever deviation a person chooses to engage in, whether it is to deviate only slightly or to deviate in a dramatic way. But the way is clear. Once he has shifted from divine revelation to human reason as the basis of authority, he can go as far as desired from historic Christian conviction, and only personal choice will determine where to stop. Thus, even those who have themselves stopped relatively close to orthodoxy are still damaging to the faith because they have opened the door to as much defection as anyone wants to engage in. Those who are coming after them will go further still. Ultimately, historic, biblical Christianity will be in shambles.

In this discussion of ultimate authority, the choice of terms is not the issue; the issue is the attitude toward Scripture itself. It is important for us to affirm that it is not necessary for one to use the term *inerrancy*. It is also vital to say that not everyone who does not affirm the inerrancy of the Scriptures is a liberal, modernist, or unbeliever. But the direction begun is a tragic step that could end in spiritual disaster.

We must reaffirm the great Reformation doctrine of *sola Scriptura*—Scripture only as our final, ultimate base of authority and truth. Anything less than this is deficient and opens the door to every conceivable kind of theological distortion. But we are getting ahead of ourselves. Certain historical developments have had a dramatic effect on the people of God. We will look briefly at these in the next chapter.

CHAPTER 2

The Dramatic Shift Away from Biblical Authority

"The destructive critics have shifted from revelation to reason. The naturalistic, uniformitarian scientists have shifted from revelation to reason. The philosophers have shifted from revelation to reason. The students of comparative religions likewise. Ultimately, all of these attacks have come because of the shift in the base of authority from revelation to reason."

THE TERRIFYING TENDENCY of many in our day to take this tragic step has not come suddenly. It has been the subtle journey of many years. Prompted by a compromising position on the Word of God, we have moved to a rationalistic base in many areas of the Christian community. How did this happen? How could people of such great confidence in the total reliability of the Scripture become people with such diluted convictions? It is important for us to trace the steps that have led to this compromising position.

Four factors caused this situation to develop. The first is in the emergence of the historical-critical approach to Scripture, a difficult area to assimilate and understand. But we must try at least to grasp the essentials. Existential philosophy is the second factor impacting modern scholars. Existentialism teaches pure subjectivity, which means that it is impossible to know objective truth. What good is an authoritative Bible if it cannot be objectively known? The third factor is the rise of naturalistic-uniformitarian science, which contends that the laws of nature reign supreme. Those who hold to naturalism see any appeal to supernaturalism as belief in the irrational. The fourth major factor is the study of comparative religions and their presumed contributions to Christianity. The outcome of this approach is *pluralism,* the view that all religions are valid ways of worship within their respective social and cultural settings. In other words, pluralists contend that God uses Islam to save the Muslim, Hinduism to save the Hindu, and Christ to save the Christian. The convergence of these four factors has presented a sustained attack against the authority of Scripture over the last century.

The Historical-Critical Approach

When examining the historical-critical approach to the Bible, it is necessary to distinguish between the various types of biblical criticism. The very term *critical* does not necessarily imply something negative. It refers to an intelligent, rational, research-oriented approach to Scripture. In itself, that is not bad. Only when it becomes destructive— rationalistic or naturalistic—is it objectionable.

We need to consider *textual criticism.* We do not have the original manuscripts of Scripture. Instead, we have many copies. It has been the task of textual criticism through the years to collate, compare, and sort through these many manuscripts, more than five thousand of them for the New Testament books alone, in order to try to restore the original text. Essentially, this has been done very satisfactorily, to the extent that we can say that the

original text of Scripture has been substantially restored. It has been frequently pointed out by many scholars that no textual variation which we are currently wrestling with affects any basic doctrine of Christianity. Most of the textual variances are of a rather minor nature, having to do with relatively insignificant matters.

Secondly, we should discuss *linguistic criticism*. This has to do with the nature of the language, particularly of the New Testament. Until the late nineteenth century, many people felt that the Greek language of the New Testament was a very special, unique Greek used only in the New Testament. It was sometimes referred to as "Holy Ghost Greek." But with the discovery of numerous papyrus documents in Egypt, it was determined that the Greek of the New Testament was the *koiné,* the common Greek used throughout the Mediterranean region in the first century. Thus, through the discovery of these letters, business documents, wills, and other writings, lexicographers were able to establish the meaning of words and the use of various idioms. This was a tremendous advance in our understanding of the New Testament language.

A third area of criticism is what we might call *literary criticism*. This area is sometimes divided into *lower criticism* and *higher criticism,* though the names are not particularly significant. They originally meant Step One and Step Two—the lower criticism had to be done before the higher criticism. Obviously, until we have a text to work with, we cannot do very much with it! Today, most critics are moving away from these terms, simply referring to this area as literary criticism. This does not deal with the integrity of the text, or the nature of the language; rather, it has to do with such things as authorship, date, occasion and place of writing, intended audience, and the basic integrity of the message itself. It also has to do with where the information

came from, the form, and how it was put together by the author. Some subdivisions under literary criticism have become quite well known in the twentieth century.

The first of these, *source criticism*, has to do with the source of the material which the author used. For example, with regard to the Pentateuch, where did the information come from? What was the source? This, of course, has given rise to a great deal of speculation. About 1753, Jean Astruc, a French physician, noted the different names of God that appear in the Pentateuch. This gave rise to the theory that two different sources were evident there: one that knew *Jehovah* as the name of God, and the other that knew *Elohim* as the name of God. Shortly after that, J. G. Eichhorn took Astruc's work and combined with it his own analysis of the styles of the various sections of the Pentateuch to come up with a theory about which portions came from one source and which came from another. This, of course, opened up a whole flood of inquiry; such men as Geddes (1792), Vater (ca. 1802), Ewald (ca. 1843), and Hupfeld (ca. 1853) made their contributions.

As a result, when the works of these men were compiled, we have essentially what is known as the documentary hypothesis of the Pentateuch—the so-called JEDP theory. According to this theory, the five books of Moses were put together from four sources—two based upon the names of Jehovah and Elohim, plus a presumed Deuteronomic source and a presumed Priestly source. All of these, ostensibly, are to be seen in the composition of the Pentateuch.

In the New Testament, much the same thing has taken place. New Testament critics began to work on the Gospel accounts, particularly the Synoptic Gospels—Matthew, Mark, and Luke—searching for the sources behind the Gospels. The popular view which finally emerged is that Mark was the original Gospel and that both Matthew

and Luke drew from Mark as one of the primary sources for their own writings. Critics used the term "Q" (for the German word *quelle,* which means "source") for what they considered as another source, made up primarily of the sayings of Jesus. Presumably, Matthew and Luke drew some of their material from this source. So we have Matthew and Luke drawing upon Mark and upon this "Q" source, plus, Matthew and Luke adding some material unique to themselves.

At this point, it should be noted that this type of procedure is not necessarily bad. It may well be that Mark was the original Gospel writer. We are inclined to think so ourselves. There may have been something like a "Q" source, although it probably consisted of a lot of oral information rather than being some document (which we have never found). Probably Matthew and Luke did add some material—Matthew, from his own eyewitness testimony, and Luke, from his own research.

But together with this source criticism there arose a basic skepticism about the reliability of the material. This is fundamental to our whole investigation. Such *destructive* literary criticism, seen particularly in source criticism and the others that we will consider presently, reevaluates the Bible as a purely human book. This whole process has sometimes been referred to as the historical-critical method.

George Ladd, in his *The New Testament and Criticism,* says, "The proponents of a thorough-going historical-critical method have insisted that historical study must be free from the restraint of any theological dogma, particularly from any doctrine of an inspired Scripture; that the biblical critic must be as open to any historical-critical conclusions as the researcher in the physical sciences must be open to the evidence of any and all facts; that any theological understanding of the Bible as the Word of God must automatically place a restraint and limitation upon the freedom of proper historical and critical investigation."[1]

Ladd goes on to say, however, that "the history of criticism shows that the proponents of a purely historical method themselves have not been motivated by a completely objective open-minded approach, but have approached the Bible with distinct philosophical and theological ideas about how it should be interpreted. In other words, their critical study was dominated by certain limiting presuppositions."[2]

What Ladd is saying, in effect, is that the historical-critical method of approaching the Scripture is basically a naturalistic, nonsupernaturalistic bias. Scripture is viewed as a purely human book and is, therefore, subject to all the foibles and problems involved with humanity. Since nobody is perfect, this view holds that no author of Scripture is perfect. Therefore, we are to look for flaws, we are to expect discrepancies, we are not surprised to find errors, we expect to find truth and untruth mixed together. In this process of study, the critical scholars say, we are to use all of the techniques of so-called scientific criticism, even as we would use them in the study of the works of Bacon, Spinoza, Shakespeare, or Milton. Thus, at the very heart of the *destructive* historical-critical methodology is the fact that the Bible must be explained in totally naturalistic terms. That, of course, colors the whole process.

Form criticism is a little different, in that it seeks to determine the literary styles that are to be found in the text. For example, with regard to New Testament form criticism, the basic question that form critics have tried to answer is, "How did the historical Jesus become the Christ of faith?" This question is based upon the assumption that the Jesus who is pictured in the New Testament is not the real Jesus who actually lived.

For the better part of the nineteenth century, critics were searching for the "historical Jesus," that is, they were attempting to go behind the actual words of the New Testament and discover the "real Jesus," the "simple carpenter," the "simple teacher." They were trying to find all of this underneath the complicated theology which, they say, somehow developed later and which was recorded in our New Testament. They attempted to separate the text into various literary units, such as narrative accounts, sayings, teachings, parables, and miracle stories.

Each one of these, they believed, was somehow derived from the faith of the early church. In other words, what was found in the life of Jesus as recorded in the Gospels was not really what Jesus did and said so much as what the early church *remembered* about what Jesus did and said, and much of this was colored by tradition and by later teaching. Therefore, they concluded, we do not have real historical documents; we have the early church's theological faith remembrances of Jesus.

The latest example of the search for the "historical Jesus" is the Jesus Seminar, a consortium of seventy-four scholars organized in 1985 for the purpose of propagating their radical conclusions about the Gospel records. The seminar met regularly to decide the genuineness of the sayings of Jesus given in the four Gospels by way of voting with colored marbles. A red marble was used to signify the vote that a saying was authentic. Sayings that were considered to be probably real were indicated with pink marbles. Belief that a statement is doubtful was signified with a gray marble. Finally, a black marble was used to express the view that a saying was never said by Jesus and therefore is fake.

Not surprisingly, the seminar concluded that very few of the sayings recorded in the four Gospels were actually said by Jesus. Virtually the entire Gospel of John was rejected.

Jesus was decreed to have never said, "I am the way, the truth, and the life. No one comes to the Father except through Me" (John 14:6), or any other similar statements. Only one saying in the Gospel of Mark was considered authentic, and in fact only fifteen sayings in all four Gospels were deemed to be genuine. By contrast, the book in which the seminar expresses the greatest confidence is not one of the four Gospels at all, but rather is a Gnostic fraud, *The Gospel of Thomas.*

The Jesus presented by the Jesus Seminar is a benign sage who preached platitudes while wandering about the Judean desert. The truth is that the members of the Jesus Seminar fell prey to the same temptation that characterized the previous attempts to recreate "the historical Jesus": they created a Jesus in their own image. The conclusions of the Jesus Seminar reveal more about the beliefs of its various members than they do about Jesus Christ Himself.

Then we have *redaction criticism.* A redactor is an editor. Therefore, redaction criticism has to do with how the writers may have put together their material. For example, whoever wrote the Gospel of Matthew was an editor, they say; he was not a historian. He was an editor and a theologian. Therefore, he picked and chose certain incidents out of the traditions of the early church about Jesus and put them together in a particular fashion so as to present a particular theological point of view. Redaction criticism attempts to determine what the writer was trying to prove. He was not just writing a history or a biography, according to this view. He was trying to prove something, and the way he put his material together will tell us what he was trying to prove.

Now, that is not altogether wrong. Obviously, the writers were trying to prove something. John said, "These are written so that you may believe Jesus is the Messiah, the Son of God" (John 20:31). But, again, it is the *negative* aspect of this approach that has become harmful. Most of the redaction critics have been rationalistic in their approach. Their thrust has not been to reproduce faithfully the theology of Christ or the theology of the new covenant, but rather it has been to attempt a negative analysis of these writers who are perceived as putting together something which satisfied them, but which was not necessarily true historically and theologically.

The next trend in the world of biblical scholarship was *genre criticism,* from the French word *genre,* meaning "kind" or "sort." Just as narrative, poetry, and biography are kinds of literature, so the *midrash* was a genre or kind of literature within the Semitic community. A midrash was a story that was used for teaching purposes. The whole point of genre criticism is to determine in each specific case what type of literature is being studied, what form it takes, what genre it is. If this can be done, we can then proceed to interpret the particular piece of literature correctly. When we ask what sort of methodology a writer has used to tell his parable or write his apocalyptic story, and how it is to be understood, and what are the principles for interpreting it, we are engaged in *genre criticism.*

When applied to the Gospels, for example, genre criticism makes the author not only a redactor, or editor, dealing with sources, but also an innovator, an originator of material. For instance, Matthew, according to these critics, was trying to present a particular theological point of view. In so doing, he put together a lot of material from the traditions concerning Jesus and His disciples. But because the material itself was not sufficient for his purposes, he made up some material himself. In other words, the Gospels are said to be of the genre midrash, in which the rabbis used to create material in order to present a point. According to this point of view, Matthew (and, presumably, Luke and

Mark) made up some events and sayings and presented them in historical form to provide the framework for the message that he was trying to present.

According to the genre critic, those who did this were not being deceitful, they were not lying, they were not trying to present something under false pretenses. They were just using an established type of literature to get a point across. If we understood the type of literature they were writing, we would not be offended by the fact that they did it in this way. Furthermore, if we understood the type of literature they were writing, we could interpret it correctly. This would relieve us of the mistaken necessity of trying to take everything in the Gospel literally, as though Jesus actually said a thing verbatim, actually did this or that, went there, saw this, and spoke these words.

Genre criticism, again, has its place, but in a very limited realm. If we can understand the type of literature that the person is writing, obviously it will help us to interpret that literature. But when we start saying that the biblical writer made up events that never occurred and created sayings which Jesus and the apostles never uttered, then the critic has gone far beyond the legitimate limits of criticism into destructive criticism, once again doing violence to the integrity of the text.

We can trace this *destructive* literary criticism back a long way. For example, the Jewish philosopher Benedict Spinoza, who lived in the seventeenth century, was a forerunner of modern higher criticism. If we browse through his writings, we will note that he points out that the Bible contains contradictions. This did not bother him. He maintained that the Bible does not contain propositional revelation, that is, actual statements of fact. As a matter of fact, he said that those who hold to such a view have set the Bible above God. Spinoza, like Bacon and Hobbes before him, taught that the authority of the Bible was purely in religious matters. He did not think that the Bible had anything to say about secular matters, and, therefore, we should not look to the Bible for answers in matters of science and history—only in matters of faith and morals. Spinoza also denied the miraculous in Scripture.

We also note the philosophy of G. W. F. Hegel (1770–1831), best known as the dialectic method. He reasoned that there is a tension between one position, the *thesis,* and a second position, the *antithesis.* As these two interact, eventually a *synthesis* (a third position) emerges, bringing into light a new aspect of reality. Then, this synthesis becomes the thesis all over again, and an opposing position, another antithesis, comes into play, resulting in a new synthesis, and on and on—sort of an evolutionary development of thought.

In the nineteenth century, F. C. Baur, who was a professor at Tübingen in Germany, applied this Hegelian philosophy to the New Testament. Briefly, his reasoning went like this: There are two contradictory strands of teaching in the New Testament. One can be identified with the apostle Paul. His is the theology of grace, the theology of salvation by faith alone. The other is the theology essentially of Simon Peter and the Jerusalem church. This is the legalistic philosophy or theology reflected in James, teaching a salvation based upon law-keeping and legalism. Ultimately, these two points of view, the thesis and the antithesis, came together into a synthesis, and that synthesis is what we finally have in the New Testament, although we can see strands of both throughout.

Baur thought that Paul wrote only four epistles. He accepted Romans, 1 and 2 Corinthians, and Galatians as being authentically Pauline. The rest he felt were not in keeping with his hypothesis; therefore, he made the facts fit his hypothesis. Although Baur's particular viewpoint is not as popular as it was a hundred years ago, it still can be seen in the thinking of many rationalistic theologians today. So we have still another philosophical strand that has affected biblical criticism.

What we see essentially is that during the seventeenth century and, with a vengeance in the eighteenth century, there developed a viewpoint that Scripture is a human book written by human beings, with the same hang-ups, the same foibles, the same fallible, inherent capabilities that all people have. Therefore, we must treat Scripture as any other book. We must apply to it all of the methods of historical criticism as we would any other book.

The latest type of criticism challenging the authority of Scripture is called *reader response criticism.* This type of criticism moves in an entirely different direction from the other critical methods we have surveyed. The previous methodologies focus on the origin of a text, while reader response criticism seeks to understand the interpretive processes that occur when a person reads a text. In short, radical reader response critics argue that it is not the author but the reader who determines the meaning of a work of literature. They contend that a text has no meaning until the reader, with his experiences and cultural conditioning, provides a text with meaning. Rather than discovering the meaning of a text, the reader supplies it. The end result is that a particular text, such as a passage of Scripture, does not have just one correct meaning. Rather, it has many possible interpretations, all of which are equally valid.

Reader response critics claim that the Bible's teachings change depending on the interpretative community of a particular reader. Therefore, when a devout Catholic reads the Bible, it teaches that Peter was the first pope; when a charismatic examines the Bible, it says that physical healing is in the atonement; and when a Baptist studies the Bible, it declares that immersion for believers is the only proper mode of baptism. Reader response critics are not merely saying that different people read the Bible differently; they are arguing that, depending upon the reader, the meaning of the Bible *itself* actually changes. They contend that their position is verified by simple observation. They then conclude that rather than debating about the correctness of any one interpretation, it is better to recognize that there is no correct interpretation—only different ways to use the text.

If it is possible for the Bible to have many meanings, all of which are "correct," then it makes no sense to talk about the final authority of the Bible. That was exactly the argument made by a reviewer who was critical of an earlier edition of this book. In his opinion, this understanding of the Bible is "the product of interaction of text with reason, experience, and tradition." Therefore, he dismisses even the possibility that the Scriptures can be the final authority in matters of faith and practice by stating, "In short, I am maintaining that there is no *sola scriptura* method."[3]

This explains why so many scholars today are unconcerned about their obvious biases when they interpret the Bible. Since everyone is biased, what difference does it make that they are, too? Therefore, many theologians today create interpretations of the Bible that are accepted as credible only to their respective interest groups. For example, feminist theologians often use reader response criticism to interpret the Bible to make it fit their agenda. Most (honest) feminist biblical scholars admit that the plain language of the Bible does not seem to endorse many of the key tenets of feminism. When the methods of reader response criticism are employed, this is no longer a problem.

After one feminist theologian described the act of Bible reading as an "open dialogue between two partners in conversation," she justified her reinterpretation of any passage that disagrees with feminism on the basis that "the authority of the canon of the Bible" must conform to the "authority of the canon of her own experiences."[4] Another feminist scholar lauds reader response criticism as "useful for feminist theological thinking" because it recognizes that "the meaning of the text is the creation of an interpretive community."[5] Used in this way, reader response criticism is the declaration of open season on biblical authority.

The truth is, the reader response method of interpreting the Bible, or something close to it, has been used in countless Sunday school classes throughout the years. After reading a passage of Scripture, well-meaning teachers, who have no idea what the principles of proper interpretation are and who have never heard of reader response criticism, ask their students, "What do these verses mean to you?" And the students' replies, even if there is no consideration of the author's intent, the intended audience, or the text's context and genre, often are all received as being equally valid. "Well, one can make the Bible mean whatever one wants it to mean," they shrug when someone confronts them with what a particular passage of Scripture actually is teaching.

A number of scholars employ reader response criticism, but they do not like the chaos that the methodology produces. Some of them are calling for a magisterial authority to restore interpretative order to how the Bible is understood. This would be a return to a view of the Bible held by Roman Catholicism (which is something that many reader response critics freely admit). The Roman Catholic Church has always held officially to the inspiration and inerrancy of the Scriptures, but at the same time it has also contended that the Roman Church is the only competent interpreter of the Bible.

During the Reformation, advocates for the Catholic Church argued against the Protestants by warning that if the Bible were made available to everyone, the result would be that there would be no consensus as to what the Scriptures actually teach. Every man would become a church unto himself and simply would do "what was right in his own eyes" (Judg. 21:25 NASB). The practical result of the Roman Catholic position is that Rome becomes the final interpretive authority. Reader response critic Stanley Hauerwas of Duke University concludes that the Roman Church was right. He declares, "The Bible is not and should not be accessible to merely anyone, but rather it should only be made available to those who have undergone the hard discipline of being a part of God's people."[6] These are strange words coming from a Protestant.

It must be pointed out that Baptists have never claimed to be infallible in our interpretation of the Scriptures. It is one thing to recognize that, because we are finite and fallen creatures, we will not have in this life a perfect understanding of the Bible, but it is another thing to claim that we are the ones who provide the Bible with meaning. To acknowledge an imperfect comprehension of the Bible is just an honest statement of the obvious, but to claim that I, the reader, am filling the biblical text with meaning borders on blasphemy. You and I do not decide what the Bible means; because *God* determined the meaning when His Holy Spirit inspired the writers!

The reader response critics commit the grievous error of replacing the Author with themselves. In this scheme the Bible is no longer the final authority; the reader is. It is troubling that the remedy advocated by some reader response theologians is the same solution proffered by

Roman Catholicism throughout the centuries: submission to a human pontiff as the final authority. This is a no solution at all for self-respecting evangelicals.

The various techniques we have discussed are not totally without value. But in the hands of a skeptic who does not accept the supernatural element in Scripture, they become very destructive and ultimately can deny the very essence of biblical Christianity. This has been one of the major thrusts against basic, biblical Christianity in the last two hundred years and more. The historical-critical method offers some good tools for Bible students, but it makes a terrible master.

Benjamin C. Fisher, former head of the Southern Baptist Education Commission, has said that "the application of scientific and linguistic analysis to the evaluation and interpretation of biblical literature brought about profound changes in our view of the historical Jesus and the trustworthiness of the Scriptures. For many people this raised serious questions as to whether the Scriptures are a gift from God or, especially in the case of the resurrection of Jesus, a wish-fulfillment of the early Christian community."[7]

Existential and Postmodern Philosophies

The second major factor contributing to the shift away from biblical authority is the rise of existential philosophy and more recently postmodernism and its application to theology. It is a matter of ongoing debate as to whether postmodernism is simply existentialism taken to its logical conclusion, or rather it should be understood as a new philosophical approach in its own right.

In classical philosophy, two views have prevailed with regard to how a person knows truth. One is the rationalistic view, which says there is something intuitive and basic in one's mind which enables us to determine truth by reasoning alone. The other is empiricism, which says that we know truth by our senses. Immanuel Kant (1724–1804), regarded by many as perhaps the most important philosopher of all time, tried to reconcile these two aspects.

In his classic work, *The Critique of Pure Reason,* Kant sought to combine rationalism and empiricism into a new epistemological system. His concept—summarized briefly and slightly oversimplified—was this: Both the rationalist and empiricist are right, but both are wrong, up to a certain point. It is true, he says, that we gain our knowledge from experience, from empirical sources. But, he says, the mind possesses basic intuitive abilities by which man arranges and catalogs the sense information which comes into the mind. So both faculties are involved—the basic abilities, the filing system furnished by the mind, and the data which comes into the mind through empirical sensation.

More important, from our standpoint, Kant concluded that no knowledge of God is possible through scientific methodology because God is above empirical investigation. Since we have no intuitive knowledge of God, the existence and reality of God must be established on some basis other than rationalism or empiricism. What was that basis? Essentially, he said (and this he carried further in two of his later works, *The Critique of Practical Reason* and *Religion within the Limits of Reason Alone*) that although religion cannot be sustained by reason or by empirical investigation, it is nonetheless valuable in our lives because of moral necessity. In other words, we need religion in order to live moral lives and to have a reasonably moral and stable society, even though it is not possible to establish its validity, either by empiricism or rationalism.

Kant had no desire to destroy Christianity. In effect, he wanted to place it beyond the reach of philosophical and scientific investigation and thus, hopefully, safe from both. But the result was quite different. His readers and hearers took him to mean that since religion cannot be substantiated either by empirical investigation or by intuitive reasoning, then God probably does not really exist. Probably there is no God and probably religion is not valid. Kant tried to salvage this by his moral argument, but was not altogether successful.

The German theologian Friedrich Schleiermacher (1768–1834) was a professor of theology at the University of Berlin. About 1800, he took Kant's philosophy and tried to bring a theology out of it. In essence, he concluded it was true that as a result of the philosophical work of Kant and the findings of the biblical critics, there probably was no way to establish the validity of Christianity. He felt it could not be established from the standpoint of an authoritative Bible, from human reason, or from empirical investigation. Nonetheless, Schleiermacher said, we must retain Christianity because it is necessary for our experience. The essence of his position was, "Let's try to retain the experience of Christianity, even though we do not have the empirical or revelational basis for it that we once thought we had."

This is where the so-called "two-story" concept comes in. Think of a two-story building. The first floor is biblical authority and revelation. The second story is Christian experience. Historically, the second floor had always been built on the first one; Christian experience had always grown out of biblical revelation and biblical authority. But now, philosophically and critically, the first floor has in effect been destroyed, and Schleiermacher was willing to concede this. But he was not willing to concede the demise of the second floor. So we have, in effect, the second floor suspended in space as by a theological skyhook.

This particular philosophy—experience without a firm basis of biblical authority—is where much of contemporary theology finds itself. It is seen very graphically in modern neoorthodoxy. Neoorthodox theologians still talk about Jesus, salvation, and faith, yet they believe that the Bible is shot through with contradictions, errors, primitive cosmologies, and pagan concepts. This is essentially what we mean by existential theology. Existential theology is a theology based on human experience rather than upon any divine revelation or divine authority. Essentially, it means that we can have the experience of God without a propositional revelation from God.

There are degrees of existential theology. There is the left wing, which might be reflected in Rudolf Bultmann. The "middle" wing might be reflected in Karl Barth and Emil Brunner. Then there is the right wing, which includes some people today who call themselves evangelicals. They tell us that they believe in Jesus, that they believe in the resurrection, that they believe in salvation through faith; but they do not believe in a completely authoritative Bible, and they do not see any necessity for such a Bible. Why? Because God, in some existential, mystical way, can speak to them through a Bible which in itself is not necessarily accurate in every respect. They do not care whether the Bible is altogether accurate or not. It is of no concern to them. All they are concerned about is their religious experience based upon an "encounter" with God through the Bible—and even through the imperfections of the Bible.

Karl Barth went so far as to say that God intentionally allowed imperfections in the Scripture so as to cause an even greater trust on the part of His people who could have faith in spite of all the imperfections. This is the ultimate in philosophical absurdity!

Where is the danger? Is it not true that we want to have a personal experience with God? Is it not true that putting it all into practice and having a genuine experience with God is more important than the minutiae and details? But that is not the point. The point is that all of it thus becomes *subjective.* It all becomes *mystical and existential.* When we begin to deny the historical, scientific, geographical, and chronological accuracy of Scripture, what logical reason do we have for retaining the "theological facts"? If it does not make any difference how accurate the Bible is, if just what God says to us through the Bible is essential, then how do we know that what He says about the atonement is necessarily factual? How do we know that what He says about the resurrection is necessarily true? Eventually, the central core of the Christian faith is replaced with some sort of a vapid, self-centered experience. That is the great danger when subjectivism and mysticism replace actual propositional revelation.

Recently existentialism has given way to *postmodernism* as the philosophical fad of the day. The subjectivism of existentialism slides inevitably to relativism, which then descends into nihilism. Nihilism denies the existence of any objective grounds for values or truth, and postmodernism is the modern philosopher's white flag of surrender in his search for truth apart from God. But rather than admit that the secular enterprise of trying to arrive at truth while rejecting biblical authority is a failure, the postmodernist declares that there was no such thing as objective truth to find in the first place. Postmodernist philosopher John Caputo sums up the position of postmodernism with eight words, "The truth is that there is no truth."[8] Perhaps you notice that his statement is self-contradictory, because if he is telling us the truth when he says that there is no truth, then he is contradicting himself (this is known as "the

Liar's Paradox"). But logical consistency is not a concern to the postmodernist.

Friedrich Wilhelm Nietzsche was the most influential nihilist of the late nineteenth century. Postmodernists agree with his definition of truth: "Truths are illusions about which one has forgotten that this is what they are."[9] It is no surprise that postmodernists reject the belief that the Bible (or any other book, for that matter) has any final or "true" meaning. Therefore, any creed or confession is denounced as "the rhetoric of oppression."

According to the worldview of the postmodernist, since there is no absolute truth, then there must be complete tolerance of all religious truth claims. In such a pluralistic framework, the only sin that still exists is "intolerance." It is important for evangelicals to remember that the early Christians were not martyred simply for worshiping Jesus as Lord. The rulers of the Roman Empire prided themselves on their acceptance of all religions. Then why were the Christians persecuted? The early church was perceived as dangerous because it held that Jesus *alone* is Lord. In pluralistic Rome, such a belief was considered to be extreme, narrow-minded, and bigoted. In a word, the early Christians were persecuted for being "intolerant."

Since today's postmodernist advocates a similar type of pluralism, it is not surprising that postmodernism views any claim of biblical authority to be equally intolerant. When "tolerance" is considered to be the greatest virtue, then any claim to hold to the final authority of truth is seen as the greatest sin. This is why conservative Christians are castigated by modern culture for our refusal to accept homosexuality as a viable lifestyle. According to the postmodernist, we are not just in error for our presumed intolerance; we are immoral.

When dealing with a postmodernist, it is possible for conservative evangelicals to strangely wish for the classic liberal of the past. In the old debates between conservatives and liberals, even though neither side thought that the other side had the truth, at least both sides agreed that such a thing as truth existed. Today, postmodernists consider "truth" to be merely a word—nothing more, nothing less. They see any attempt to adhere to the final authority of the Bible to be a grab for power and an attempt to control others. Postmodernists see truth claims entirely in political terms, and that "truth" is used as a weapon by those in positions of authority to oppress the weak.

One disturbing trend is the level of acceptance of postmodern thinking among the young people in conservative churches. Recently a study was conducted in which teenagers who attend Bible-believing churches were surveyed. An alarming 53 percent agreed with the statement, "There is no such thing as absolute truth."[10] This may explain why today many young people react so indifferently to any kind of truth claim. The challenge posed to biblical authority by postmodernism is obvious. The attack is not just on the truthfulness of the Bible, but on the very concept of truth itself.

Naturalistic, Uniformitarian Science

The third challenge to basic biblical Christianity is the rise of naturalistic, uniformitarian science. Uniformitaranism, essentially, means that the universe operates now as it has always operated. There are universal principles that have always been in operation. There has been no intervention or interruption by anything or anyone supernatural.

This development in virtually every field of science took place concurrently with the growing acceptance of the historical-critical method in biblical studies and the evolution in philosophy that has just been described. The early champions of naturalistic, uniformitarian science were James Hutton and Charles Lyell. In 1830, Lyell set forth in his *Principles of Geology* an explanation of geology that did not depend upon any supernatural element. Everything in geology could be explained totally on the basis of natural causes without supernatural intervention. Charles Darwin in 1859 in his *Origin of Species,* and in 1871 in his *Descent of Man,* picked up that same basic uniformitarian thinking and applied it to the study of biology.

This same uniformitarianism has been applied in the social sciences as well—Sigmund Freud, for example, applied it in the area of psychology, and Emile Durkheim did the same in sociology. Freud believed that "God" is simply an extension of human need. Man grew up with a human father, and he depended upon him to meet most of his needs. When it was no longer possible for his human father to meet his needs, he created a cosmic father. So God, according to Freud, is simply that which we create out of a psychological need.

Durkheim and others in the area of sociology said that "God" was simply a figment of man's imagination, intended to explain that which is unexplainable, and to placate that which they feared. What man could not control—such as fire, wind, flood, the sun and moon—he tended to worship and sought to appease. When everything is viewed from a naturalistic standpoint, God and the Bible are essentially eliminated. This has given rise to the whole evolutionary theory that is so prominent in our day and has done away with any concept of divine creationism or of humans created in the image of God. Evolutionary biologist Richard Dawkins proclaimed that "although atheism might have been logically tenable before Darwin,

Darwin made it possible to be an intellectually fulfilled atheist."[11] This obviously has had tremendous effect upon biblical Christianity, presumably discrediting significant portions of Scripture entirely because they do not agree with this uniformitarian, naturalistic, skeptical, essentially atheistic, position.

Most proponents of atheistic naturalism generally cannot live with the logical conclusions of their position. Darwinism teaches that vicious selfishness is the primary force motivating all life on earth, yet few evolutionists believe that a civilization based on such an operating paradigm could thrive or should exist. All but the most ardent naturalists agree that a society based on the principle of "survival of the fittest" is somehow wrong, but they cannot tell you why. Despite the best efforts of atheists such as Freud, Durkheim, and more recently Dawkins, Darwinian evolution does not and cannot explain such things as human knowledge, morality, or the concepts of beauty, goodness, and truth.

Today, some of the strongest opposition to philosophical naturalism comes from members of the scientific community. Microbiological researchers such as Michael Denton and Michael Behe demonstrate that uniformitarian theories about origins cannot explain the complexity found in even the most basic life forms. Philosophers and logicians like Alvin Plantinga and Phillip Johnson reveal the irrationality in naturalism and the logical holes in Darwinism. Scientists as diverse as Kurt Wise and Hugh Ross point out the overwhelming evidence that the universe is the product of a wise and loving Supreme Being. Despite the claims of Richard Dawkins, science does not provide intellectual cover for atheism.

Presumed Contributions of Comparative Religions

The fourth major factor in breaking away the confidence in the total reliability of the Scriptures is the study of comparative religions and their presumed contributions to Christianity. The basic idea here is that unbelieving scholars, in their study of the other religions and human traditions, have found similarities between these religions and the Judeo-Christian beliefs. They have concluded that religion has evolved on the earth just like everything else and that our concept of deity is evolving and emerging; starting all the way back at the beginning with primitive animism and polytheism, over many, many generations, monotheism has finally developed. Christianity is now, presumably, the highest form of monotheism, they say. Nonetheless, Christianity has been shaped by all of the other human religions and thus is not to be considered unique; it is simply a more refined and developed view of God, morality, and ethics.

Here are two or three examples. There is an ancient account of creation from the Babylonian tradition which is called the Enuma Elish. It probably dates several hundred years earlier than Genesis, yet there are some remarkable similarities. In both accounts the earth, following creation, is said to be empty and void. There follows, in the Babylonian account, an essentially similar order of events, from a watery chaos to the eventual "rest" of the deity. The number seven is prominent—the seven days of creation in Genesis are matched by the seven cantos or tablets in the Enuma Elish. Yet there are striking differences. For instance, the Genesis account presupposes monotheism, whereas the Babylonian account presupposes a gross polytheism.

A second example is the Babylonian flood account, the Epic of Gilgamesh. Again, it is very similar to the Genesis flood account and was probably written at least two hundred years earlier than Genesis. The great flood is planned by the gods. The impending catastrophe is revealed to the hero. In the Gilgamesh story, the hero is Utnapishtim; in the biblical account, it is Noah. In both accounts, the flood is connected with the defection of the human race. In both, the hero and his family are delivered by means of a huge boat and special blessings are conferred on the hero after the flood subsides. But again, there are striking differences. We have monotheism in the Genesis account but polytheism in the Gilgamesh story. Genesis is on a high moral plane, while immorality, even among the gods, characterizes the Babylonian account.

How do we explain this? Here are Babylonian accounts of creation and the flood which admittedly predate Genesis by at least two centuries. The rationalistic critic says that there is only one way to explain this—admit that the Genesis account was drawn from the Babylonian story and was changed somewhat to make it more compatible with the religion of Israel. Thus, we must not look upon the Jewish Scriptures as being particularly unique. They are simply adaptations from the writings of other cultures and religions which were synthesized, modified, and added to until the formation of what we call the Old Testament.

Here is a New Testament example: the Golden Rule. "Whatever you want others to do for you, do also the same for them" (Matt. 7:12), which Jesus taught in the Sermon on the Mount. The critics point out to us that Hinduism has a Golden Rule, Buddhism has a Golden Rule. Likewise, Zoroastrianism, Confucianism, Taoism, Greek philosophy—all have a Golden Rule. All of these predate the enunciation of the Golden Rule by Jesus, so what is so unique about the Christian version?

What about the miraculous birth and the miraculous preexistence of Jesus? Critics say there is nothing so unusual about these claims either. In Buddhist literature, Gautama the Buddha is said to have had a miraculous birth. The same is claimed for Lao-tze, founder of Taoism. So also Mahavira of Jainism and Zoroaster of Zoroastrianism. All of these, along with Jesus, are said to have had a supernatural origin and were in some way related to the gods.

Rudolf Bultmann made a great deal of the so-called "Gnostic redeemer myth." Here was folklore in the first century, he says, that was very similar to the biblical accounts and was ultimately picked up by the Christian writers.

All of this, they say, is proof that Christianity is not unique, that Jesus is not unique, that it is all a product of the cultures, the traditions, and the civilizations which went before and which existed simultaneously with Judaism and Christianity. This has had a profound effect upon how biblical Christianity is regarded today, and it has driven many people away from traditional biblical theology.

We need to point out essentially how these similarities are to be accounted for, though we cannot do that in great detail here. Concerning the creation and flood accounts, there are two ways of understanding the phenomena. It is theoretically possible, from a naturalistic standpoint, that the Genesis accounts are derived from the Babylonian stories.

That, however, does not make a great deal of sense, even from a purely scholarly point of view, because a derivation is normally less than the original, not more— less simple, less noble, less inspiring than the original, not greater. It is not very likely that one would take an account and raise it to the majesty of Genesis by drawing from the rather dreary, polytheistic, immoral narratives of the Babylonians. It is much more likely that the biblical explanation is the right one—that there really was a divine creation and a flood, and that when Moses recorded what we now have in Genesis, he wrote down something that actually occurred and furthermore that he wrote it by divine inspiration. If the creation and the flood really took place, we would expect memories of these to filter down through all peoples and all civilizations, including the ancient Babylonians.

Therefore, it is not surprising that they have in their tradition stories of a creation and a flood, because those things actually happened and the stories were passed down orally from generation to generation. But not being preserved by divine revelation, they became garbled.

When we come to such things as the origin of the founders of the world religions, it is true that there is a Buddhist tradition that Gautama, who lived hundreds of years before Jesus, was also miraculously born. But if we will check it out very carefully, we will find that the particular Buddhist writings which record this were not written until after Jesus was born. The same thing is true of Lao-tze, Confucius, Zoroaster, and Mahavira. Although some of these people lived long before Jesus did, the commentaries which bring their stories into approximate conformity with the Christian story were not written until after Jesus. So hundreds of years after Gautama lived, some of his Buddhist followers began to read back into his story some of the facts which were picked up and borrowed from Christianity. In other words, it is just the opposite of what the rationalists are saying: It is not that Christianity borrowed from these religions; these religions borrowed from Christianity.

Concerning the Golden Rule, this was undoubtedly a part of God's original revelation to the human race, preserved in varying forms by differing peoples. Once again, it all depends on one's presupposition. If we begin with the idea that there was no creation, that there is no God, that there is no such thing as the supernatural, that there is no divine revelation, then we are forced to some conclusions simply because there seems to be no other alternative. But if we start with the biblical framework of a creator God and a revealer God, then all of these things begin to fit together into a very different explanation. This skepticism over the last one hundred and fifty years has been very destructive to biblical Christianity.

One consequence of the rationalistic approach to comparative religions is the view that, contrary to what Jesus Himself taught in John 14:6 ("I am the way, the truth, and the life. No one comes to the Father except through Me"), Christ is not the only way to be reconciled to God. This position is advocated in two forms either as pluralism or more cautiously as inclusivism.

Pluralism is the view that all the world religions, such as Hinduism and Buddhism, are valid expressions of religious truth within their respective social and cultural environments. This notion teaches that Islam saves the Muslim just as Christ saves the Christian. Pluralism is the prevailing view among many people in the liberal mainline denominations.

Inclusivism is closely associated with pluralism, and it is making inroads among evangelicals. An inclusivist believes that Jesus Christ saves everyone who is saved, even if he or she does not realize it or acknowledge it. Therefore, the devout Muslim or the earnest Buddhist is being saved—without his or her knowledge—by the blood of Christ. This is why some inclusivists refer to adherents of other religions as "holy pagans" and "anonymous Christians."

Inclusivists do not consider themselves to be pluralists, but many of the results of their teachings are the same as that of pluralism. A clear example of this is their understanding of the purpose of missions. No longer is missions seen as the charge to preach the Gospel to a dark and dying world. Both the pluralist and the inclusivist believe that the majority of people in the world will go to heaven whether they ever hear the gospel or not. Therefore, the task of missions is no longer seen as the seeking of the lost but the locating of the redeemed. How different this outlook is from the viewpoint of the New Testament (Acts 4:12)!

These areas of concern represent a significant but mostly overlooked shift from divine revelation to rationalism as the ultimate base of authority. The destructive critics have shifted from revelation to reason. The naturalistic, uniformitarian scientists have shifted from revelation to reason. The philosophers have shifted from revelation to reason. The students of comparative religions, likewise. Ultimately, all of these attacks have come because of the shift in the base of authority from revelation to reason.

This has led, first of all, to religious experience without theological foundation—the two-story effect we mentioned earlier. We now have around us in rationalistic circles, in neoorthodox circles, and in quasi-evangelical circles (which are really still neoorthodox) the idea that religious experience can survive without an authoritative revelation from God in Scripture. *It cannot ultimately survive!* But there are those who are trying to place it on that basis. The great emphasis is on experience as being the measure of truth: If I have had a real experience that "blesses" me, they say, then it must be right regardless of what the Scripture says. Such theology leads away from God, not toward God.

This has also led to relativistic ethics, so-called "situational ethics." If there is no propositional revelation from God, if there are no direct commands from God, then, obviously, there are no moral absolutes. This has led to the whole gamut of aberrations in the area of ethics. We might point out here that if there is no authority from God, if there are no moral absolutes, then we have no certainty about anything. The secular humanists are saying that society can exist successfully without any word from a now-and-then deity, or as one writer has said, "without benefit of clergy." But it cannot ultimately exist successfully.

How do we know that we ought to restrain murder? Or that murder is wrong? Or that rape is wrong? Or that armed robbery is wrong? Or that embezzlement is wrong? Doesn't everyone know that these are wrong? No, everyone does not know they are wrong. There are many people in our prisons who apparently did not know they are wrong. If we do not have any moral absolutes, then we cannot establish that something is wrong. Some say we establish it by common consensus. But suppose the consensus changes, as it apparently did in Nazi Germany when it was considered proper to perpetrate the tragic massacre of the holocaust. All of this results from a lack of moral absolutes.

Then, finally, all of this leads to a so-called evangelism without any biblical concept of man's actual condition or God's revealed response. Even the rationalists and the neoorthodox talk about evangelism. But they are not talking about the same thing that biblical Christians are talking about. They do not have any basis for biblical evangelism. They do not think that people are actually lost, or that there is a hell or eternal punishment. They do not think there is need for or reality in a substitutionary atonement. Many of them do not believe there was a bodily resurrection of Jesus Christ. Therefore, to them, evangelism becomes quite a different thing.

We need to be cautious that while we are talking of going on with evangelism and missions, those with whom we are speaking have the same thing in mind that we do. Some denominations, once great for God, are talking about evangelism and missions, but they mean something quite different. And they show the effects of this devastating shift away from biblical authority which, as we have seen, is a contradiction of biblical Christianity. Without an authoritative divine revelation, worship degenerates into mere form and ritual, ministry concerns itself only with the temporal and the physical, and authority becomes the result of human ingenuity rather than the mind of God.

It is vitally important for us to examine the positions taken on the authority of the Bible by the early Church Fathers and by our Protestant forbears. We will turn our attention to these two historical areas now, taking note of how their views on authority impacted the church's witness and missionary effectiveness.

CHAPTER 3

The Church's Historical Position on Biblical Authority

"Look carefully into the Scriptures which are the true utterances of the Holy Spirit."

—CLEMENT OF ROME, CA. A.D. 100

THERE IS MUCH discussion today about the historical belief and practice of the church regarding the nature of Scripture. It is routine for those who believe in the full authority of Scripture—that is, biblical inerrancy—to be characterized as ultraconservatives, as bibliolaters (those who worship the Bible rather than God), as those who make the Bible a paper pope. It is claimed that the doctrine of biblical inerrancy is a recent development, that it derives from post-Reformation scholasticism and that it does not have its roots in the Church Fathers and in the mainstream of Christian theology.

A book by Jack Rogers and Donald McKim, *The Authority and Interpretation of the Bible: An Historical Approach*, attempted to document this particular position. The authors claimed that modern-day evangelicals have departed from the historic understanding of the church

43

with regard to the nature of Scripture and as a result have caused confusion and division within the body of Christ today. (For a complete and scholarly refutation of this position, refer to the subsequent work by John Woodbridge, *Biblical Authority*.) It is our purpose in this chapter to demonstrate rather briefly that the Christian church down through the centuries has believed in the full authority of Scripture and that modern-day evangelicals who continue to support this view of Scripture are in the mainstream of Christian orthodoxy. Actually, those who have departed from this position are the ones who have introduced novelty into the Christian church and who are causing division within the body of Christ.

One of the earliest of the Church Fathers, outside of the apostles themselves, to write anything which has been preserved for us today was Clement of Rome (who died in A.D. 102). Clement said, "Look carefully into the Scriptures which are the true utterances of the Holy Spirit." Even from this very brief quotation, there can be no doubt that Clement understood the Scriptures to be inspired by the Holy Spirit of God and thus to be absolutely reliable.

Justin Martyr (ca. 105–165), one of the most famous of the early Christian apologists, said, "We must not suppose that the language proceeds from the men who are inspired but from the divine word which moves them." Justin also said, "The history which Moses wrote by divine inspiration . . . the Holy Spirit of prophecy taught through him." Surely there can be no doubt concerning Justin's position with regard to the full inspiration of Scripture or of the Mosaic authorship of the Pentateuch.

Irenaeus, bishop of Gaul in the late second century A.D., was also unambiguous in his statements concerning Scripture. "All Scripture as it has been given to us by God will be found to be harmonious." Again, he said,

"The Scriptures are perfect, inasmuch as they were uttered by the word of God and His Spirit, though we want the knowledge of their mysteries." Again, Irenaeus, although admitting that we are not always capable of interpreting Scripture perfectly, nonetheless clearly states his belief in the perfection of Scripture as originally written.

Clement of Alexandria (A.D. 150–217) said this about Scripture: "There is no discord between the law and the gospel, but harmony for they both proceed from the same author." Again, Clement said, "Of which [the Scriptures] not one tittle shall pass away without being accomplished for the mouth of the Lord, the Holy Spirit, spoke it." Clement, too, expresses his complete confidence in the divine origin of Scripture and its complete accuracy.

Clement's colleague, Origen (A.D. 185–253), also of Alexandria, was clearly unambiguous in his view of Scripture. "We cannot say of the writings of the Holy Spirit, that anything in them is useless or superfluous, even if they seem to some obscure." In another place Origen said that the Scriptures "breathe the spirit of fullness and there is nothing whether in the law or in the prophets, in the evangelists or the apostles which does not descend from the fullness of the divine majesty." Again, Origen said, "Believing that the divine foreknowledge which supplies superhuman wisdom to the race of man by the Scriptures, has placed, so to speak, the seeds of saving truth in each letter."

The opponents of biblical inerrancy in the twentieth century have tended to ridicule the so-called "domino theory," that is, that if any error at all can be found in Scripture, the credibility of all Scripture will be damaged. It is interesting to note that this theory did not originate with the twentieth century. Consider this quote by the church father, Cyprian (died A.D. 258): "The gospel cannot stand in part and fall in part." We will see that he was not the only father of the church who expressed concern in this area.

Athanasius (died A.D. 373), the great defender of Christian orthodoxy at the Council of Nicea in A.D. 325, said, "In the words of the Scripture is the Lord." A reading of his contest with Arius at the Council of Nicea will demonstrate that he used the full authority of Scripture effectively in his argument concerning the full deity of Jesus Christ.

Augustine (A.D. 354–430), considered by many to be the greatest theologian of the ancient church, was also quite clear in expressing his views concerning the integrity of Scripture. "Only to those books which are called canonical have I learned to give honor so that I believe most firmly that no author in these books made any error in writing. . . . I read other authors, not with the thought that what they have taught and written is true, just because they have manifested holiness and learning." Note that Augustine explicitly states that no author of any biblical book made any error in writing. How does this differ from the modern definition of biblical inerrancy? The answer is that it does not differ in any sense whatsoever. On another occasion, Augustine said, "Therefore, we yield to and agree to the authority of the Holy Scripture which can neither be deceived nor deceive."

Jerome (A.D. 342–420), also one of the great scholars of the early church, is perhaps most famous as the translator of the Latin Vulgate edition of the Bible. Jerome stated, "When you are really instructed in the divine Scriptures and have realized that its laws and testimonies are the bonds of truth, then you can contend with adversaries, then you will fetter them and lead them bound into captivity, then of the foes you have made captive, you will make free men of God." Obviously, Jerome believed the Scriptures to be absolutely authoritative and thus valuable in their use against the enemies of Christianity.

Thomas Aquinas (A.D. 1225–1274) is considered by most Christians to have been the most influential theologian of the Middle Ages. What was his view of Scripture? Consider the following section from his writing:

> However, sacred doctrine makes use of these authorities [philosophers] only as extraneous and probable arguments. Properly, theology uses the authorities of the canonical Scripture as the necessary argumentation. The authority of the doctors of the church is properly employed but as merely probable, for our faith rests upon the revelation given to the apostles and prophets who wrote the canonical books and not on revelation (if there be such a thing) made to other teachers. Whence, Augustine said in his letter to Jerome, "Only to those books which are called canonical have I learned to give honor so that I believe most firmly that no author in any of these books made any error in writing. I read other authors, not with the thought that what they have taught and written is true, just because they have manifested holiness and learning."

Note that Thomas Aquinas agreed precisely with the position of Augustine whom we quoted earlier. Representing as he does the theological attitude of the medieval church, does not his writing demonstrate that the church in that era held to the full authority and inspiration of Holy Scripture as did the early church?

Let us move on to the time of the Protestant Reformation. Martin Luther (A.D. 1483–1546) was absolutely clear and precise concerning his view of biblical inspiration despite the attempts of many today to muddy the waters concerning Luther's theology. Consider some of his prominent statements. "This is our foundation where the Holy Scripture establishes something that must be believed, there we must not deviate from the words as they sound, neither from the order as it stands unless an express article of faith (based on clear Scripture passages) compels us to interpret the words otherwise, or arrange them differently. Else, what would become of the Bible?"

The following quote indicates that Luther also held to a "domino theory." "They do not believe that they [the words of Scripture] are God's words. For if they believed they were God's words, they would not call them poor, miserable words but would regard such words and titles as greater than the whole world and would fear and tremble before them as before God Himself. For whoever despises a single word of God does not regard any as important."

Or consider the following statement from Luther:

"Whoever is so bold that he ventures to accuse God of fraud and deception in a single word and does so willfully again and again after he has been warned and instructed once or twice will likewise certainly venture to accuse God of fraud and deception in all of His words. Therefore, it is true, absolutely and without exception that everything is believed or nothing is believed. The Holy Spirit does not suffer Himself to be separated or divided so that He should teach and cause to be believed one doctrine rightly and another falsely."

Certainly, Luther was a man of plain speech, and it is difficult indeed to misinterpret the precise thought that he expresses in these words, that is, that Scripture is the Word of God and if one rejects any of it, he is, in effect, rejecting all of it. This is the essence of Protestant, Reformation theology.

John Calvin (A.D. 1509–1564), the father of Presbyterian and Reformed theology, is likewise unambiguous in his statements concerning Scripture. At varying places in his writings, he refers to Scripture as "the sure and infallible record," "the inerring standard," "the pure word of God," "the infallible rule of His holy truth," "free from every stain or defect," "the inerring certainty," "the certain and unerring rule," "the infallible word of God," "inviolable," "infallible oracles." These are hardly the statements of a man who believed that the Scriptures contained error.

Consider also what is generally thought to be Calvin's classic statement on Scripture:

> When it pleased God to raise up a more visible form of the church, He willed to have His word set down and sealed in writing. . . . He commanded also that the prophecies be committed to writing and be accounted part of His word. To these, at the same time, histories were added, also the labor of the prophets but composed under the Holy Spirit's dictation. I include the Psalms with the Prophecies. . . . That whole body, therefore, made up of law, prophecies, psalms and histories was the Lord's Word for the ancient people.
>
> Let this be a firm principle, no other word is to be held as the Word of God, and given place as such in the Church, than what is contained first in the Law and the Prophets, then in the writings of the apostles. . . . [the apostles] were to expound the ancient Scripture and to show that what is taught there has been fulfilled in Christ. Yet, they

were not to do this except from the Lord, that is, with Christ's Spirit going before them and in a sense dictating their words. . . . [They] were sure and genuine penmen of the Holy Spirit and their writings are therefore to be considered oracles of God and the sole office of others is to teach what is provided and sealed in the Holy Scriptures.

Calvin also said:

In order to uphold the authority of Scripture, he [Paul] declares it to be divinely inspired. For if it be so, it is beyond all controversy that men should receive it with reverence. . . . Whoever, then, wishes to profit in the Scriptures, let him first of all lay down as a settled point this—that the law and the prophecies are not teachings delivered by the will of men, but dictated by the Holy Ghost. . . . Moses and the prophets did not utter at random what we have from their hand, but since they spoke by divine impulse, they confidently and fearlessly testified, as was actually the case, that it was the mouth of the Lord that spoke. . . . We owe to the Scripture the same reverence which we owe to God, because it has proceeded from Him alone.

Can there be any question about John Calvin's commitment to total biblical authority and inerrancy? Absolutely not!

One of the most influential preachers and theologians of the early American scene was Jonathan Edwards (A.D. 1703–1758). Along with George Whitefield, Edwards was a leader in the Great Awakening of the eighteenth century, which shaped to no small degree the early political and cultural development of our nation. His view of Scripture can be seen in the following statement:

> The Scriptures are evidence of their own divine authority as a human being is evident by the motions, behavior and speech of a body of a human form and contexture, or, that the body is animated by a rational mind. For we know no otherwise than by the consistency, harmony and concurrence of the train of actions and sounds, and their agreement to all that we can suppose to be a rational mind. . . . So there is that wondrous universal harmony and consent and concurrence in the aim and drift such as universal appearance of a wonderful, glorious design, such stamps everywhere of exalted and divine wisdom, majesty, and holiness in matter, manner, contexture and aim, that the evidence is the same that the Scriptures are the word and work of a divine mind; to one that is thoroughly acquainted with them, as 'tis that the words and actions of an understanding man are from a rational mind, to one that is of a long time been his familiar acquaintance.

These selected quotations from some of the most prominent and influential of the Church Fathers indicate beyond any doubt that a belief in the full integrity and accuracy of Scripture has been an integral part of the church's belief from the very earliest times. Now we turn our attention to our own particular heritage as Baptists, to see what a brief review of Baptist history has to teach us concerning our historic position on the doctrine of Scripture.

CHAPTER 4

Baptists' Historical Position on Biblical Authority

"Did the inspired writers receive everything by direct revelation?
The inspired writers learned many things by observation or inquiry,
but they were preserved by the Holy Spirit from error; whether in
learning or in writing these things."

—JOHN BROADUS

ALTHOUGH HISTORIANS ARE not unanimous concerning the origin of the people whom we today know as Baptists, most Baptist historians would probably agree that the roots of our modern Baptist movement are to be found in the sixteenth- and seventeenth-century Protestant Reformation. Many Christians who were dissatisfied with the Roman Catholic system began a movement of purification from any trace of that tradition. These people became known as Puritans. For a time they remained in the Church of England, but later they became disillusioned and decided to form their own assemblies. As such, they became known as Separatists. Eventually, they became known as Baptists because of their firm belief in believer's baptism for adults.

Most Baptist historians would identify the first Baptist church to be the one established in Amsterdam in 1609. The leader of that church was John Smyth, a highly educated man with both bachelor's and master's degrees from Cambridge University. What was Smyth's view of Scripture? He leaves no doubt in our minds as this quotation from *Baptists and the Bible* shows:

> Men are of two sortes, Inspired or ordinary men. Men Inspired by the Holy Ghost are the Holy Prophets and Apostles who wrote the holy scriptures by inspiration. 2 Peter 1.21, 2 Tim. 3.16, Rom. 1.2, namely the Hebrue of the ould testament and the greeke of the New Testament. The holy scriptures viz. the originalls Hebrew and Greek are given by Divine Inspiration and in their first donation were without error, most perfect and therefore Canonicall.[1]

It is instructive to note that not only did Smyth believe in the full inspiration of Scripture, but he also clearly distinguished between the original manuscripts of Scripture and the copies and translations which came later. Many are telling us today that there is no precedent for distinguishing between the original manuscripts and the editions which we have today. Notice, however, that one of the first Baptists clearly made that distinction, and that distinction has been observed and recognized down through the generations since his time, as we shall see.

At about the same time John Smyth was leading the church at Amsterdam, another early Baptist, Thomas Helwys, was authoring a confession of faith (1611) entitled *A Declaration of Faith of English People Remaining at Amsterdam in Holland*. Most Baptist historians regard this as the first English Baptist confession of faith. Notice the doctrine of Scripture contained in that confession:

> That the Scriptures off the Old and New
> Testament are written for our instruction, 2 Tim.
> 3.16 and that we ought to search them for they
> testifie of CHRIST, Jo. 5.39. And therefore to bee
> used with all reverence, as conteyning the Holie
> Word off God, which onclie is our direction in all
> things whatsoever.[2]

Note that Helwys was seemingly unaware of the modern distinction between the so-called "theological" content of Scripture and the so-called "secular" content of Scripture. He said that Scripture "is our direction in all things whatsoever." Presumably, this would mean science, history, chronology, and geography as well as theology.

Another prominent seventeenth-century Baptist clergyman was Thomas Grantham (1634–1692). His view of Scripture is clearly set forth in this quotation:

> We therefore conclude that such hath been the
> Providence of God, that Men could not corrupt
> those Holy Writings which he had ordained for
> the Generations to come; neither can all the Art of
> Evil Men rase out, or foist into the Greek copies,
> so much as one Sentence, but either Friend or Foe
> would soon detect them.[3]

It should be obvious that Grantham agreed with Helwys and Smyth concerning the inspiration of Scripture.

The Second London Confession (1688–1689) is one of the more influential Baptist statements of faith. It is the Baptist revision of the famous Westminster Confession which became the founding theological document of the Presbyterian and Reformed churches. The statement on holy Scripture is very extensive, but two brief excerpts will capture the flavor of the statement. "The Authority of the Holy Scripture for which it ought to be believed dependeth not upon the testimony of any man or Church; but wholly upon God (who is truth itself) the Author thereof; therefore it is to be received, because it is the Word of God."

Again, "The whole Councel of God concerning all things necessary for His own Glory, Man's Salvation, Faith and Life is either expressly set down or necessarily contained in the Holy Scripture; unto which nothing at any time is to be added, whether by new Revelation of the Spirit, or traditions of men."[4]

It is simply beyond controversy that the early English Baptists believed in the full authority and integrity of Scripture. Indeed, we could say they believed in the complete inerrancy and infallibility of Scripture.

When we move to the new world, the name of Roger Williams is well-known among seventeenth-century Baptists. Williams is famous for his stand concerning the separation of church and state and the persecution that subsequently resulted. Consider this statement from Williams concerning Scripture:

> I urge that this will of God (for this declaration of what Christ said and did and of all the rest of the Scripture was a Declaration and Revelation of God's Will to his People and to the whole World) this written and revealed will of God I said was the Judge and Decider of all Questions, the tryer of all Spirits, all Religions, all Churches, all Doctrines, all Opinions, all Actions.[5]

Notice once again that Williams refused to limit the authority of Scripture to theological and ethical matters alone. Scripture, according to Williams, was the final arbiter of all matters concerning human existence.

When we move to the eighteenth century, perhaps the most influential Baptist theologian is John Gill of Northamptonshire, England. Gill also was very clear in his statements concerning the authority and inspiration of Scripture, and he too made a clear distinction between the original manuscripts of Scripture, which he referred to as the "original exemplar," and the modern editions. According to Gill, every translation must be checked out by the original editions and thus corrected and amended as necessary. He said, "And if this was not the case, we should have no certain and infallible rule to go by; for it must be all the translations together, or some one of them, not all of them because they agree not in all things: not one; for then the contest would be between one nation and another which it should be, whether English, Dutch, French."

Gill went on to point out that the Roman Catholic Church made a grave mistake in adopting the Latin Vulgate as the official version of Scripture because the Vulgate, he says, "abounds with innumerable errors and mistakes." How could such an unreliable translation be superior to the original manuscripts themselves! He did concede, of course, that our translations are on the whole adequate to produce salvation and to be the basis for the Christian life. Nonetheless, ultimate authority must be sought in the originals.[6]

One of the influential Baptist educators of the nineteenth century was Francis Wayland, who became president of Brown University. His view of Scripture is captured in the following statement:

There has seemed to me a growing disposition to omit the proof of a revealed truth from revelation, and to attempt the proof from every other source than the Bible. Why should this be? If the Bible be true, why should we ignore its evidence? To do thus may seem more philosophical, and may be more pleasing to unregenerate men, but is it really according to the mind of the Spirit? Do we not thus practically lead men to the conclusion that there is a higher authority than the Word of God, by which it is to be judged and to which its teachings are to be subjected?[7]

Wayland saw clearly that to suggest that the Bible is in error at any point is to suggest that there is some authority that is more accurate than Scripture and which can be used to correct Scripture. This again reflects his fear of the shift from divine revelation as ultimate authority to one's own rational thoughts as ultimate authority.

One of the most influential leaders of Baptists in the southern United States in the nineteenth century was John L. Dagg. He was the first truly "Southern Baptist" theologian. In one of his theological treatises, he says this concerning Scripture: "It cannot be that wicked men conceived so pure a system; that by every utterance which they made they condemned their own fraud; and that they have preserved others from perpetrating like iniquity by denunciations so terrible that the very imagination of them is unwelcome to the minds of transgressors. The Holy Bible cannot be the work of unholy deceivers."

He went on to point out that the good men who wrote the Bible were not liars. Thus, when they claimed that the Bible is "inspired of God," or "the commandments of the Lord," they must be understood to be accurate in those statements. They were men of integrity. He said, "But a careful examination of the inspired word has not only served to repel the charge of reconciling the apparent discrepancies, but it is added new proof that the Scriptures were written by undesigning and honest men without any collusion and that there is perfect harmony in their statements, even when apparently most discordant."

Again Dagg says:

> A candid mind, after contemplating the overpowering evidences of Christianity, would decide that the alleged disagreements of the evangelists cannot furnish a valid objection to the Divine origin of the religion, even if the apparent disagreements could not be harmonized. But patient investigation converts these apparent inconsistencies into undesigned coincidences and finds in the very ground of infidel cavils, a firm foundation for Christian faith.[8]

Notice that Dagg would not support the modern opinion that we should not propose any view of Scripture until we have been able to work out all of the problems and all of the apparent discrepancies in Scripture. Dagg says that we must accept Scripture at face value because of the divine endorsement even though we are currently unable to work out every problem to our satisfaction.

It is particularly interesting to note the expressed views of early Southern Baptist educators concerning Scripture. When Southern Baptists decided to establish a seminary in 1858, three of the founding professors were John A. Broadus, James P. Boyce, and Basil Manly, Jr. If we can determine their views concerning Scripture, we can ascertain what was the original doctrinal position of the Southern Baptist Theological Seminary.

Consider this statement by Boyce concerning Scripture:

It must come from God, the source of all our
other knowledge. No other could give it, and it is
fit that no other should do so. It must be suited to
our present condition, confirming the truth already
known, and teaching what is practically useful to
man as a sinner before God. It must be secured
from all possibility of error, so that its teachings
may be relied on with equal, if not greater,
confidence than those of reason. It must come with
authority, claiming and proving its claim to be
the word of God, who has the right to command,
and to punish those who disobey his command,
with authority also, that man may with confidence
believe and trust the promises and hopes of pardon
and peace it may hold out.[9]

Basil Manly said:

This full recognition of the human authorship of
the Scriptures is of prime importance; for much of
the force of the argument against a strict doctrine
of Inspiration consists in proving this human
authorship of the sacred writings, which we think
is undeniable, and then inferring from that their
fallibility. "Human, therefore fallible," they say;
"fallible, therefore false in some measure." But this
favorite line of argument seems to us to be more
plausible than powerful. It is a mere assumption
that their being human forbids their being also
divine; that God cannot so inspire and use a
human being as to keep his message free from
error; that the human origin, under divine control,
necessarily involves either falsity or fallibility.

This seems to be perfectly plain: yet this fallacy underlies whole pages of vigorous denunciation and confident appeal.[10]

This argument, which Manly so competently disposes of, is still current today. We are asked, How can the Scriptures be the product of human beings and still be inerrant? Manly gave the answer which is still as appropriate today as it was then, that is, that God is capable of inspiring people so as to keep His message free from error. This is what the church and Baptists have believed historically.

John Broadus, perhaps the most honored name in early Southern Baptist education, prepared a catechism in which we can easily see his view of Scripture.

Did the inspired writers receive everything by direct revelation? The inspired writers learned many things by observation or inquiry, but they were preserved by the Holy Spirit from error; whether in learning or in writing these things.

What if inspired writers sometimes appear to disagree in their statements? Most cases of apparent disagreement in the inspired writings have been explained, and we may be sure that all could be explained if we had fuller information.

Is this also true when the Bible seems to be in conflict with history or science? Yes, some cases of apparent conflict with history or science have been explained quite recently that were long hard to understand.

Has it been proven that the inspired writers stated anything as true that was not true? No; there is no proof that the inspired writers made any mistake of any kind.[11]

One could scarcely ask for a plainer and more explicit statement of the current position of biblical inerrancy. John Broadus was an inerrantist in the fullest sense of the word.

No review of Baptist history would be complete without some reference to Charles Haddon Spurgeon (1834–92), the famous London preacher. He, too, dealt with the charge that if the Bible was written by genuine human beings, then the Bible must contain error. He said:

> One might suppose that believers in Plenary Inspiration were all idiots; for their opponents are most benevolently anxious to remind them of facts which none but half-witted persons could ever forget. Over and over they cry, "But there is a human side to inspiration." Of course there is; there must be the man to be inspired as well as the God to inspire him. Whoever doubted this? The inference which is supposed to be inevitable is— that imperfection is, therefore, to be found in the Bible, since man is imperfect. But the inference is not true. God can come into the nearest union with manhood, and he can use men for his purposes, and yet their acts may not in the least degree stain his purposes with moral obliquity. Even so he can utter his thoughts by men, and those thoughts may not be in the least effected by the natural fallibility of man.[12]

Spurgeon, then, perhaps the greatest of all the modern Baptist preachers, built his ministry unashamedly and absolutely upon the total authority of holy Scripture.

Not only were the founders of Southern Baptist Theological Seminary believers in biblical inerrancy, but the founder of Southwestern Baptist Theological Seminary was an inerrantist also. B. H. Carroll was as outspoken as

Spurgeon in his stand on Scripture. "It has always been a matter of profound surprise to me that anybody should ever question the verbal inspiration of the Bible," he said. "The whole thing had to be written in words. Words are signs of ideas, and if the words are not inspired, then there is no way of getting at anything in connection with inspiration. . . . What is the object of inspiration? It is to put accurately in human words, ideas from God. . . . When you hear the silly talk that the Bible 'contains' the word of God and is not the word of God, you hear a fool's talk. I don't care if he is a Doctor of Divinity, a President of a University covered with medals from universities of Europe and the United States, it is fool's talk. There can be no inspiration of the book without the words of the book."

Carroll also distinguished carefully between the original manuscripts of Scripture and the copies which we have today. "Let me say further that only the original text of the books of the Bible is inspired, not the copy or the translation. Second, the inspiration of the Bible does not mean that God said and did all that is said and done in the Bible, some of it the Devil did and said. . . . The inspiration means that the record of what is said and done is correct. It does not mean that everything that God did and said is recorded. It does not mean that everything that is recorded is of equal importance, but every part of it is necessary to the purpose of the record, and no part is unimportant. One part is no more inspired than any other part." Some are saying today that we have a "progressive inspiration." This idea is foreign to our Baptist forefathers as shown by this quote from Carroll.[13]

Perhaps the most famous theologian to be associated with Southwestern Seminary, which B. H. Carroll founded, was W. T. Conner, who spent some thirty-nine years teaching at that institution. He retired in 1949. Conner believed that the Bible was an inspired book and that it was given altogether by God. Perhaps his most explicit statement is this: "Dr. Warfield is probably correct when he says that this means that God produced or caused the Scriptures. New Testament writers (and speakers) regard God as the author of Old Testament sayings and teachings (Mark 12:36; John 10:35; Heb. 1:5; 3:7 et al.). The Scriptures then, are God's work. He produced the Scriptures."[14]

"Dr. Warfield," of course, was B. B. Warfield, the well-known Princeton theologian of the late nineteenth century who was a champion of biblical authority and inerrancy. Conner obviously agreed with Warfield.

The Baptist Faith and Message and the "Criterion Loophole"

Throughout its history the Southern Baptist Convention has had three versions of its statement of faith, the Baptist Faith and Message. The first version was adopted in 1925 in the midst of the fundamentalist-modernist controversy surrounding the theory of evolution. In 1963, a second version was approved after an outcry erupted over a commentary on the Book of Genesis that was written by a professor at Midwestern Baptist Theological Seminary. The latest edition of the Baptist Faith and Message was approved by the Southern Baptist Convention at Orlando, Florida, in June 2000 in order to correct shortcomings in the 1963 statement.

The first section of the 1925 Baptist Faith and Message makes the following statement about the Bible:

> We believe that the Holy Bible was written by
> men divinely inspired, and is a perfect treasure
> of heavenly instruction; that it has God for its
> author, salvation for its end, and truth, without any

mixture of error, for its matter; that it reveals the principles by which God will judge us; and there is, and will remain to the end of the world, the true center of Christian union, and the supreme standard by which all human conduct, creeds and religious opinions should be tried.

Note that the 1925 statement makes clear claims about the source, character, purpose, and authority of the Bible. As to its source, the human aspects of the Bible are acknowledged, but its divine authorship is emphasized. The character of the Bible is described as perfect ("perfect treasure") and inerrant ("without any mixture of error"). This characterization of the Scriptures is borrowed from the British philosopher John Locke, who in 1702 said of the Bible that it had "God for its author, salvation for its end, and truth, without any mixture of error for its matter."

The 1925 statement declares that the purpose of the Bible is to serve as a guide to salvation ("salvation for its end") and service ("it reveals the principles by which God will judge us"). This means that the Bible must be the final authority in matters of faith ("supreme standard by which . . . creeds and religious opinions should be tried") and practice ("all human conduct"). The 1925 statement is a concise confession of the historic position of Baptists concerning the Bible.

The original Baptist Faith and Message served the Southern Baptist Convention for over thirty years. However, by the late 1950s there was a growing concern that many in leadership positions of the denominational agencies and schools held to a lower view of Scripture than that proscribed by the Baptist Faith and Message. Then in 1961, Ralph Elliott, professor of Old Testament at Midwestern Baptist Theological Seminary, published with Broadman

Press a commentary entitled *The Message of Genesis,* which questioned the Mosaic authorship of the Pentateuch. When Elliott republished the commentary after being instructed not to do so by the trustees, he was dismissed in the fall of 1962. To resolve the resulting crisis, a committee was formed to study the issue and, if necessary, provide revisions and clarifications to the Convention's statement of faith. The outcome of their work was a second version of the Baptist Faith and Message, which was approved in 1963. However, the new statement contained the infamous "criterion loophole."

To understand what the criterion loophole is, and how it was used, it is necessary to note the changes made from the 1925 statement to the 1963 version in the section on the Bible. The 1963 Baptist Faith and Message retained the claim that the Bible had "truth, without any mixture of error, for its matter." But the section concluded with the sentence, "The criterion by which the Bible is to be interpreted is Jesus Christ." What the 1963 statement gave with the right hand of inerrancy, it took away with the left hand of interpretation theory.

Using this seemingly innocuous statement, several seminary professors used the neoorthodox tactic employed by Karl Barth of placing the revelation of Jesus Christ in opposition to the rest of the Bible. That is, if the Bible teaches something that seems to be difficult to reconcile with the teachings of Jesus, or if the Scriptures give instructions about an issue that Jesus did not address, then the Bible is wrong in those areas. However, this argument ignores two important facts. First, the Bible is where we learn about Christ. Thus, the revelation of Jesus Christ cannot be separated from the Bible because it is located in the Bible. Second, proponents of the loophole claim that Jesus is the criterion by which we interpret the Bible, but then they ignore what Jesus actually says about the Bible. Jesus never considered His teaching to be at variance with the rest of Scripture. He certainly did not have a low view of Scripture. The Savior sums up His assessment of the Bible in John 17:17: "Your word is truth."

In addition to the criterion loophole, the 1963 statement describes the Bible as being "the record of God's revelation of Himself to man." Neoorthodox professors interpreted this to mean that the Bible itself is not the revelation of God, but that it contains the revelation of God. Therefore in their view, the Bible is a human book, replete with all the frailties and foibles of a human work, but nonetheless possesses the revelation of God somewhere inside. Who, then, is to determine whether a particular passage of Scripture is inspired or not? Why, neoorthodox seminary professors, of course!

There are many examples that show that this type of thinking is being employed by some Southern Baptist leaders. From the various choices let us examine one instance of the moderates' approach to each of the Testaments that illustrates their use of the criterion loophole. For a good example of a neoorthodox handling of the Old Testament, one needs to look no further than the two-day dialogue that occurred between the moderate and conservative factions of the Southern Baptist Convention in Birmingham at Samford University in October 1990. Walter Harrelson told about his Aunt Zora, who was his Sunday school teacher when he was eight or nine. He held her up as a model of a good Bible teacher and as an example of a practitioner of the criterion loophole. He stated, "But now and again, when the Bible depicted some extraordinarily cruel act of God against, say, the Canaanite population (Josh. 10:40–43; 11) or the Midianites (Num. 25; 31), Aunt Zora would say, 'Well, children, that's what the Bible says, and it must be true. But you know, there's something wrong somewhere, for God is not like that.'"[15]

He commented approvingly, "God is not like that. The Bible itself led Aunt Zora to a recognition that the biblical writers, who faithfully preserved the record of God's sacred teaching and saving deeds, sometimes must have misunderstood or slipped." Note Harrelson's use of the criterion loophole: If a passage in the Bible portrays God in a way that seems difficult to reconcile with the revelation of God in Jesus Christ, then that passage must be wrong.

An example of the criterion loophole being used in the handling of the New Testament is the way in which some Southern Baptists justify ordaining women for the pastorate. Specifically, some neoorthodox Southern Baptists place the revelation of Jesus Christ in opposition to the instruction given by Paul to Timothy in 1 Timothy 2:9–15. During the debate over the 2000 version of the Baptist Faith and Message concerning the role of women in the home and the church, one moderate argued that Jesus sanctioned women pastors. He stated, "On the day of Jesus' resurrection, the heart of the gospel, Jesus commissioned women to go and declare His resurrection to adult men and order them to come meet Him as their resurrected Lord (Matt. 28:10; John 20:17)."[16] This, he contended, was an example of women in positions of spiritual leadership. Therefore, Paul's prohibition against women being in spiritual authority over men "was Paul's temporary practice as the church started, but it was never intended to be God's highest will for His church for all ages."

Another editor of a Baptist state paper, while arguing for the merits of the criterion loophole in the 1963 Baptist Faith and Message, maintained that Paul contradicted himself as to the role of women in the home and the church.[17] The editor's solution? He was sure that Christ would be in favor of permitting women pastors, and since Jesus is the criterion by which we interpret the Scriptures, Jesus trumps Paul. This editor used the criterion loophole to determine that the apostle Paul was wrong—not on the basis of what Christ actually taught—but on the basis of what the editor believed that Jesus would have taught.

In response to the practice of setting the teachings of Jesus in opposition to the remainder of the New Testament, it should be pointed out that this approach ignores several important points. First, Paul wrote his instructions on the role of women in the church and home long after the earthly ministry of Christ. If Jesus was intending to teach something contrary to 1 Timothy 2:9–15, the apostolic church failed to grasp it. To the contrary, the firmest teachings about women in ministry occur at the end of the apostolic era. The early church did not understand Jesus' actions the way moderates do, nor do we see the Holy Spirit correcting the apostles on this matter anywhere in the Bible (which is something He did on occasion about important matters; see Acts 10–11).

Second, moderates are not consistent in their treatment of the apostle Paul's writings. They do not disregard the rest of Paul's instructions in 1 Timothy as culturally conditioned. For example, they do not reject Paul's assertion in 1 Timothy 2:4 that God desires the salvation of all men. Why? They like that verse.

Third, the advocates of the criterion loophole cannot give any biblical example of the New Testament believers using a similar method to reject any of the teachings of the apostles. To the contrary, the early church understood the apostolic ministry to be the continuation of the teaching of Jesus Christ through the abiding work of the Holy Spirit (John 16:12–15).

The fourth point to make is that the statement, "Jesus Christ is the criterion by which we interpret the Bible," has traditionally been understood to mean that one should ask how any given passage points to Jesus or how a passage relates to what the Bible teaches about Jesus. Using the methods of neoorthodoxy, the moderates turn this principle on its ear. Instead of treating a passage as universally normative unless the Bible teaches otherwise, they treat a text as culturally conditioned unless explicitly sanctioned by Christ. This way, the silence of Jesus on the role of women in ministry is used to negate what is clearly taught elsewhere in the Bible.

Finally, although moderates do not like this being pointed out, they are not the only ones who use the silence of Jesus on a particular issue as an excuse for rejecting what the rest of the Bible plainly teaches. Many who argue that evangelicals should change their stance on homosexuality do so on the grounds that Jesus never condemns it. Using the "criterion loophole," pro-gay advocates contend that the prohibitions against homosexuality given by Moses and Paul are culturally conditioned and are not to be considered normative. Moderates, by and large, do not like having their hermeneutical methods associated with the approaches of those advocating the acceptance of homosexuality as a viable lifestyle, but it does not change the fact that they are both employing the same logic.

It is clear that the "criterion loophole" is a way in which lip service can be paid to the Bible's inspiration while sidestepping its authority. Using this loophole, some have claimed to hold to a high view of Scripture while at the same time they have denied its applicability. It is not that they deny that a particular text is inspired; rather, they deny that its teaching is normative.

Historically, Baptists have believed that all the teaching of Scripture is to be accepted as normative unless the Bible itself limits the audience. The advantage of this method is that it acknowledges the Bible as the final authority. Not only is this the historical position of Baptists; it is also the way the Bible treats itself. The "criterion loophole" is a rejection of the ultimate authority of Scripture.

At the Southern Baptist Convention in 2000, a third version of the Baptist Faith and Message was adopted in which the criterion loophole was deleted. The sentence "The criterion by which the Bible is to be interpreted is Jesus Christ," was changed to "All Scripture is a testimony to Christ, who is Himself the focus of all divine revelation." Also, where the 1963 statement says that the Bible "is the record of God's revelation of Himself to man," the phrase "the record of" was omitted in the 2000 Baptist Faith and Message to read that the Bible itself "is God's revelation of Himself to man."

A vigorous debate preceded the passage of the new statement of faith. Virtually all of the discussion at that meeting focused on the changes made to the section concerning the Bible. At one point in the discussion, one of those opposed to the new Baptist Faith and Message stated, "The Bible is a book that points toward the truth. With that being said, the Bible is still just a book. Christians are supposed to have a relationship with Jesus Christ, the living Word, not a book." With his statement, "the Bible is still just a book," an audible gasp could be heard throughout the convention center. Never had a moderate so clearly stated his opinion regarding the Scriptures on the floor of the annual meeting. After twenty years of debate and disagreement, the one real issue had come to the fore: whether or not Southern Baptists would recognize the Bible as being the inerrant and final authority.

In these two chapters, then, we have demonstrated that the view of the church down through the centuries, almost without exception, until recent times, has been that the Bible is the authoritative, infallible, inerrant Word of God and that it is our sole source of authority in every given area of human understanding. We have seen that this is true of Baptists as well as other Christians. Perhaps we could summarize this section by means of a quotation from Kirsopp Lake, late professor of theology and philosophy at Harvard University:

> It is a mistake often made by educated persons who happen to have but little knowledge of historical theology, to suppose that fundamentalism is a new and strange form of thought. It is nothing of the kind. It is the partial and uneducated survival of a theology which was once universally held by all Christians. How many were there, for instance, in Christian churches in the eighteenth century who doubted the infallible inspiration of all Scripture? A few, perhaps, but very few. No, the fundamentalist may be wrong. I think that he is. But it is we who have departed from the tradition, not he, and I am sorry for the fate of anyone who tries to argue with a fundamentalist on the basis of authority. The Bible and the corpus theologicum of the church are on the fundamentalist's side.[18]

This quote reminds one of the story about the farmer and his wife who were driving to town in their pickup truck. The farmer was sitting behind the wheel in silence and his wife was sitting against the door, as far from her husband as she could get, also in silence. After several miles, the wife said, "Jed, when we were first married, we didn't sit this far apart."

Jed's reply was, "I ain't moved."

The facts show that current evangelicals who are intent on maintaining the church's dedication to the full authority of Scripture are in the mainstream of Christian history and tradition. It is those who would dilute the authority of Scripture and who have been polluted by liberal and neoorthodox theology, who have introduced novelty into the church. They are the ones who are responsible for the confusion and divisiveness which have resulted. They are the ones who have moved.

CHAPTER 5

The Bible Speaks About Itself

"Are we claiming more for the Bible than it claims for itself when we say the Scriptures are inerrant?"

HAVING REVIEWED THE historic position of the church concerning biblical authority, we must now turn our attention to what the Bible says about itself. In much of the debate concerning whether the Scripture contains error or not, very little attention is given to what the Bible claims for itself, and especially what Jesus Christ had to say about Scripture. Some today are saying that inerrantists actually claim more for the Bible than the Bible claims for itself. For example, we occasionally hear someone say, "Where does the Bible use the term *inerrant?* If the Bible does not use that term itself, what right do we have to use the term or to urge others to affirm it?" This is a very superficial argument, but it has appeal to some people.

In the first place, we must point out that Christians have used a number of theological terms for centuries that do not occur in Scripture. The word *Trinity* nowhere occurs in Scripture—but the doctrine of the Trinity certainly is clearly taught. The term *hypostatic union,* referring to the union of the divine and human natures of Christ, nowhere appears in Scripture—but the doctrine appears clearly in Scripture. It is a cardinal doctrine of Christianity that Jesus Christ was a perfect, sinless man and genuine deity at the same time, and thus became our perfect sacrifice for sin.

It is not a good argument to claim that because a term does not appear in Scripture it is an invalid term. Whether we use the term *inerrant,* or *infallible,* or *authoritative,* or *completely accurate*—whatever term we choose to use—what we really want to know at this point in our investigation is whether or not the Bible claims this for itself. It would be a tragic mistake for us to claim *more* for Scripture than Scripture claims for itself. It would be equally tragic, however, for us to claim *less* for Scripture than Scripture claims for itself.

In reviewing what Scripture says about itself, let us begin with the Old Testament. There are several primary passages from the Pentateuch, and, assuming the Mosaic authorship of these books, these will give us information as to what Moses, the first inspired penman, thought about Scripture.

Exodus is an appropriate place to begin. "Then Moses said to the LORD, 'Please, Lord, I have never been eloquent, neither recently nor in time past, nor since You have spoken to Your servant; for I am slow of speech and slow of tongue.' The LORD said to him, 'Who has made man's mouth? Or who makes him mute or deaf, or seeing or blind? Is it not I, the LORD? Now then go, and I, even I, will be with your mouth, and teach you what you are to say'" (Exod. 4:10–12 NASB). This passage states plainly that God gave to Moses the words he was to speak; it thus implies that what He inspired Moses to say and to write was without error.

Further on in the Book of Exodus we read, "Then the
LORD said to Moses, 'Write down these words, for in
accordance with these words I have made a covenant with
you and with Israel'" (Exod. 34:27 NASB). Once again,
Scripture reveals that what Moses wrote was the Word of
God, perfect and intact.

In Deuteronomy we find another clear statement. "You
shall not add to the word which I am commanding you,
nor take away from it, that you may keep the commandments of the LORD your God which I command you"
(Deut. 4:2 NASB). This is a very explicit statement of
God's authority in His revelation.

Finally, Deuteronomy describes how God views a
prophet and the importance of communicating the Word
of God accurately. "But the prophet who speaks a word
presumptuously in My name which I have not commanded
him to speak, or which he speaks in the name of other
gods, that prophet shall die" (Deut. 18:20 NASB). Thus, it
would have been foolish for Moses to presume to add to
or take away from what God had sovereignly commanded
him to speak and to write.

It is important to recognize that throughout the
Pentateuch there are literally hundreds of references such
as, "Thus says the Lord," "The Lord said," and "The Lord
spoke." There can be no doubt that Moses claimed to be
communicating the actual words of Jehovah God.

Consider Isaiah as a typical representative of the pro-
phetic books. Some twenty times in the Book of Isaiah
there are claims that his words are the words of the Lord.
One of the best illustrations is, "Hear the word of the
LORD, you rulers of Sodom; give ear to the instruction of
our God, you people of Gomorrah" (Isa. 1:10 NASB).

Jeremiah, more than one hundred times, states that "the
word of the Lord came unto me . . ." or something similar.

For example, "To whom the word of the LORD came in the days of Josiah the son of Amon, king of Judah, in the thirteenth year of his reign. . . . Now the word of the LORD came to me saying . . ." (Jer. 1:2, 4 NASB).

Ezekiel, in more than sixty places, claims that his words are God's words and thus to be received as such. "Moreover, He said to me, 'Son of man, take into your heart all My words which I will speak to you and listen closely. Go to the exiles, to the sons of your people, and speak to them and tell them, whether they listen or not, "Thus says the Lord GOD"'" (Ezek. 3:10–11 NASB).

Daniel declares that he heard "the sound of his words; and as soon as I heard the sound of his words, I fell into a deep sleep on my face, with my face to the ground" (Dan. 10:9 NASB). Daniel was thus responding to and reporting that which he had heard directly from God Himself.

Each of the twelve minor prophets reflects in an unambiguous and specific way that he was writing the very Word of God as it came to him from Jehovah God Himself. Compare Hosea 1:1, Joel 1:1, Amos 3:1, Obadiah 1, Jonah 1:1, Micah 1:1, Nahum 1:12, Habakkuk 2:2, Zephaniah 1:1, Haggai 1:1, Zechariah 1:1, and Malachi 1:1. The prophets, without doubt, believed that they were recording the very words of God when they spoke or wrote.

In the poetic books, David emerges as the most prominent representative author. The 119th Psalm is a classic expression of the power, beauty, and inerrancy of the Word of God. Verse 89 summarizes David's thoughts regarding the accuracy of the Word of God, "Forever, O LORD, Your word is settled in heaven" (NASB). What a classic statement of David's concept of the Word of God. For those who would like to pursue David's thoughts further, the entire 119th Psalm deals with the truthfulness and the purity of the Word of God.

As we turn to the New Testament to see what it says about Scripture, several key passages are determinative. Paul writes: "All Scripture is inspired by God and is profitable for teaching, for rebuking, for correcting, for training in righteousness, so that the man of God may be complete, equipped for every good work" (2 Tim. 3:16–17). The word translated "given by inspiration of God" (Greek, *theopneustos*) means "God-breathed." *Theos* is the Greek word for God, and *pneustos* is from the word *pneuma*, which means "air," "wind," or "breath." Thus the combination of the two Greek words means "God-breathed." God breathed in (and out) of the sacred writers of Scripture what He wanted them to write, and thus it was God's Word, complete and without error. A holy and perfect God could not conceivably produce error in His Word! The goal was that the man and woman of God might be mature, completely equipped for every good work. Thus, we see that God has "breathed" the Scriptures through us with the result that all Scripture is profitable for us in a practical, day-to-day application. Without the God-breathed Scriptures we would have no absolutes for the Christian life.

When we join these words of Paul with those of Peter, we have an excellent view of just what inspiration involves. "First of all, you should know this: no prophecy of Scripture comes from one's own interpretation, because no prophecy ever came by the will of man; instead, moved by the Holy Spirit, men spoke from God" (2 Pet. 1:20–21). Holy men, set apart to God, were "borne along" by God, writing down what God wanted them to say. Peter states plainly that the biblical prophets did not make up Scripture, but that God directed them as to how and what they should communicate. Thus, the accuracy of the revelation would be according to God's standard, which is perfection.

As Peter wrote this passage, he was probably remember-
ing the Sea of Galilee where he had worked as a fisherman
before the Lord's touch upon his life. The Greek word
pneuma not only means "breath"; it also means "spirit"
or "wind." Peter had often sat in that little fishing boat in
the middle of the sea, waiting for the *pneuma* to come up
and catch his sail and take him back to Capernaum. This
was a common experience to Peter. So, by inspiration, he
uses this analogy to demonstrate just what happened in the
process of inspiration. The holy *pneuma,* the Holy Spirit,
the holy "breath" of God, moved the inspired penman
along toward the desired destination just as the physical
pneuma, the wind, moved the sailors in the boat across the
sea to the desired destination.

Before we move on to what Jesus said about the
Scripture, note briefly three other passages from the New
Testament that bear upon this matter. Peter states, "Since
you have been born again—not of perishable seed but
of imperishable—through the living and enduring word
of God. For all flesh is like grass, and all its glory like
a flower of the grass. The grass withers, and the flower
drops off, but the word of the LORD endures forever. And
this is the word that was preached as the gospel to you"
(1 Pet. 1:23–25). How can one read these words and
doubt that Peter regarded the spoken and written revelation of God as eternal and perfect?

Another well-known passage is found in Hebrews. "For
the word of God is living and effective and sharper than
any two-edged sword, penetrating as far as to divide soul,
spirit, joints, and marrow; it is a judge of the ideas and
thoughts of the heart" (Heb. 4:12). These words explain
why the Bible is not always a pleasant book to read. People
find it hard to read because it is the Word of God and,
being alive and active, it penetrates and lays open their

innermost being. This supernatural characteristic of the Word of God gives evidence of its divine origin and thus its perfection.

Finally, James declares, "By His own choice, He gave us birth by the message of truth so that we would be a first-fruits of His creatures" (James 1:18). The Word of God was God's means of bringing us to the truth, and it is itself truth (John 17:17).

With this review of the New Testament authors before us, let us look now at what Jesus Himself had to say about Scripture. We will consider Jesus' view of Scripture from several different standpoints. The place for us to begin is to ask, "Did Jesus Himself regard the Scripture as inerrant?" The answer is an unequivocal yes. He believed it to be inerrant. Consider, first of all, how Jesus treated the Old Testament passages as statements of fact. The Gospel writers recount that Jesus frequently based an argument on details found in the historical narratives of the Old Testament. For example, when the disciples were criticized for plucking grain on the Sabbath, Jesus defended them by pointing to the instance of David entering the tabernacle to take the showbread (Matt. 12:3–4). At another time Jesus condemned the Pharisees by contrasting their indifference and unbelief with the spiritual inquiries of the Queen of Sheba in Solomon's day (Matt. 12:42). These are just two of the many similar examples that can be found in the four Gospels. Therefore, to deny the historical accuracy and reliability of the Old Testament is to accuse Jesus of building his arguments on a false basis. We find throughout the Gospels that Jesus referred to and treated all references to the Old Testament as being factual, chronological, historical material. There seemingly was not a doubt in His mind that what He was referring to was accurate. He spoke of Abel, Noah, Abraham, Moses, Lot, Sodom, Solomon,

Jonah, Zechariah, and others as historical people and places.

Second, Jesus used the Old Testament as the final arbiter in all matters of faith and conduct. Whenever He was contending with the scribes and pharisees, Jesus referred to the Word of God as absolutely authoritative. In Matthew 5:17–20, Jesus said, "Don't assume that I came to destroy the Law or the Prophets. I did not come to destroy but to fulfill. For I assure you: Until heaven and earth pass away, not the smallest letter or one stroke of a letter will ever pass from the law until all things are accomplished. Therefore, whoever breaks one of the least of these commandments and teaches people to do so will be called least in the kingdom of heaven. But whoever practices and teaches these commandments will be called great in the kingdom of heaven. For I tell you, unless your righteousness surpasses that of the scribes and Pharisees, you will never enter the kingdom of heaven."

Jesus denied that He had any thought of destroying Scripture (as some charged). The Jewish leaders themselves understood that the Word of God was the final court of appeal, but they had distorted it by adding their own traditions. Compare also Matthew 22:29 and 23:2–3 for further evidence of Jesus' complete confidence in the Old Testament Scriptures.

Third, Jesus viewed the Old Testament as predicting His own life and ministry. How could this be so without divine inspiration? For example, in John 5:39, Jesus said, "You pore over the Scriptures because you think you have eternal life in them, yet they testify about Me." He was, in effect, stating, "You use the Scriptures as your source book, and yet you are unable to see the fulfillment of prophecies that relate to me as the Messiah." Other passages that reflect the same understanding are

Luke 4:21; 18:31–33; 24:27. Compare also Mark 14:21; Luke 22:37; and Matthew 26:53–56.

Fourth, Jesus expressly stated the authority of the Old Testament and of His own words. In John 10:35, our Lord said, "If He called those to whom the word of God came 'gods'—and the Scripture cannot be broken." Although some have tried to evade the force of those words, it is very obvious that Jesus Christ regarded the words of Holy Scripture as absolutely inviolable!

A second passage for consideration is that found in Mark: "Heaven and earth will pass away, but My words will never pass away" (Mark 13:31). It is difficult to conceive of a more explicit statement of the absolute authority of Jesus' words, which words were subsequently recorded in Scripture.

It is important to see that Jesus preauthenticated the New Testament Scriptures; that is, by His own statements He marked out the apostolic writings as fully inspired *before they were written.* Consider what He says in John 14:26: "But the Counselor, the Holy Spirit, whom the Father will send in My name, will teach you all things and remind you of everything I have told you." In John 16:12–14, Jesus declares, "I still have many things to tell you, but you can't bear them now. When the Spirit of truth comes, He will guide you into all the truth. For He will not speak on His own, but He will speak whatever He hears. He will also declare to you what is to come. He will glorify Me, because He will take from what is Mine and declare it to you." Christ thus makes provision for the Scripture which was yet to be written, that is, the New Testament. Matthew 16:18–19 also refers to the authority of Christ Himself which was to be entrusted to the apostles so that they would be able to carry out the divinely appointed responsibilities. "And I also say to you that you are Peter, and on this rock I will build My church, and the forces of Hades will not overpower it. I will give you the keys of the kingdom of heaven, and whatever you bind on earth will have been bound in heaven, and whatever you loose on earth will have been loosed in heaven."

Having reviewed what the Lord Jesus Christ Himself said about Scripture, a crucial question emerges that must be answered. Can evangelicals be truly evangelicals and deny Jesus' own expressed view of Scripture? If Jesus believed in the inerrancy of Scripture (and He certainly did), how can presumed evangelicals speak in terms of Jesus as Lord and reject His view of Scripture? This is, perhaps, the most important consideration that we must face in the entire discussion of inerrancy. Evangelicals make a great deal out of the fact that Jesus is Lord. If Jesus is Lord, then, by definition, that means that He is Lord of all of life. He is Lord in every area and avenue of life. It is a contradiction in terms for us to acknowledge Jesus as Lord, on the one hand, and then reject His lordship in some particular area. The point is this: If Jesus really believed in biblical inerrancy, then we need to believe in biblical inerrancy, because He said so and He is Lord! Even if there are some seeming discrepancies which we have not yet been able to work out, if Jesus said the Bible is inerrant and if He firmly believed it Himself, then we must believe it or else reject His authority and His lordship.

This logically brings up the question of what is called "circular reasoning." Someone will undoubtedly say that, philosophically, we are reasoning in a circle. We are making a big thing about the fact that Jesus believed in biblical inerrancy, and thus we must believe in biblical inerrancy because He did. But all that we know about Jesus' position on Scripture is contained in Scripture. Therefore, they say, we have to presume biblical inerrancy in the first place in order to know what Jesus said about anything. Then, we take what He presumably said about Scripture and use it to urge others to believe in inerrancy as well. In other words, we could be accused of using the Bible to prove the Bible.

Many evangelicals have confronted this problem in a very satisfactory manner, and we will briefly outline the most effective approach, that is, the principles of historiography. How do historians determine whether an ancient document is genuine or bogus? Over the years they have developed a measuring stick that can be applied to any historical document to determine whether its contents are to be accepted as fact or rejected as fiction. *Such a test will not prove scriptural inerrancy,* but it will give us an acceptable indication that the New Testament documents really do reflect actual people, events, and statements, arising from the first century A.D.

Briefly, the point is this: We can escape the problem of circular reasoning by moving back for a moment from the whole question of biblical inspiration and inerrancy and inquiring about the essential accuracy of Scripture, based solely upon the principles of historical investigation and criticism. When any document comes to us from some point in history, the historian who works with the document must have some means of evaluating and determining its reliability and its integrity. The New Testament documents, and particularly the Gospels, are no different. They can be subjected to the tests of historical criticism. Essentially these tests are two—external and internal.

The external test deals with the genuineness of the document itself. Does it actually come from the period represented? Is it a forgery? Do we have an original document or is this an accurate copy of the original? This essentially is the problem of textual criticism.

Basically, the internal test covers such matters as the ability of the primary witnesses to tell the truth. What about competence, degree of attention, the danger of leading or loaded questions? Is the primary witness *willing* to tell the truth? Was there bias? Who are the intended hearers? What literary style is used? What about the laws and conventions of the time in which the document was written? Is the primary witness reported accurately with regard to the detail under examination? Is there independent corroboration?

Applying these tests to the New Testament documents, we can establish the basic veracity of our Lord's statements, apart from theological considerations. We are then on solid ground in taking the statements of Jesus concerning biblical accuracy and regarding them as essentially accurate. And, if they are essentially accurate, and He did indeed declare that Scripture is inerrant, is totally reliable, and cannot be broken, then it is our final court of appeal. By this particular methodology we can escape the problem of circular reasoning and come right back to the major point. If Jesus really did regard the Bible as being inerrant and infallible, how can any person who calls himself a Christian take any other view?

To support this a little further, there is widespread agreement among prominent *liberal* theologians that Jesus did, in fact, believe in the full authority of the Scripture. For example, H. J. Cadbury of Harvard Divinity School, F. C. Grant and John Knox of Union Theological Seminary, Adolf Harnack and Rudolf Bultmann, two of the most famous of the German theologians, all agreed that Jesus, without question, believed as the rabbis of His day believed, that Scripture is totally without error, totally authoritative and reliable.

To a man, all of these liberal theologians believed that Jesus was mistaken, but they nonetheless admitted that such was His belief. If this is what Jesus believed, how can we believe anything differently? The liberal mind can claim that Jesus is wrong, but we evangelicals cannot. Therefore, we are put in this very demanding position of either affirming biblical inerrancy as Jesus did or else contradicting the very authority of the One whom we call Lord.

However, should we not be "inductive" in our approach? There are those within the evangelical camp who are saying that the scholarly thing to do would be to maintain an inductive approach to the evidence. What they mean is this: Let us not go off the deep end, let us not go off half-cocked and state dogmatically that Scripture is inerrant, when, as a matter of fact, we have not checked it out completely to determine if it is inerrant. In other words, what we ought to say is that we believe that it *may* be inerrant but we are waiting until all the data are analyzed before we can make that as a final, dogmatic statement.

What this means is that as long as there is a single apparent discrepancy in the biblical account, we cannot definitely and dogmatically say that Scripture is inerrant, because it just might prove otherwise. Therefore, scientifically, inductively, we should be cautious and "scholarly" and wait until all the evidence is in before we come up with the final pronouncement.

That simply will not do! If we wait until all the "evidence" is in, we will wait until the Second Coming of Christ! By then, it will be too late for us to affirm our belief in the inerrancy of Scripture. We say again, the main reason we accept the inerrancy of Scripture is not because we have all of the problems worked out, not because we can reconcile every difficulty, but simply because Jesus Himself said so and we believe Him because Jesus is Lord!

There is one other consideration we must examine. That is the area of God's holiness. Essentially, the question arises, "Can a holy God inspire an errant Word?" If the Bible is considered to be the Word of God in any meaningful sense, can a holy, perfect, righteous God inspire something which is imperfect, unholy, and full of errors, imperfections, and false information? Whatever God does, He does perfectly. That is the answer to this basic question. The fact that God has used human beings does not mean that He cannot produce a perfect Word. Using their imperfections, their personalities, their vocabulary and literary style, He nonetheless has produced something perfect which will not lead astray and will not deceive those who depend upon it.

Chapter 6

Biblical Authority: What We Do and Don't Mean

"The doctrine of inspiration simply says that God the Holy Spirit superintended. He overruled their particular imperfections, and did not allow these imperfections to intrude into the Scripture that they wrote."

WHEN WE TALK about biblical authority and inspiration, what do we mean? The more liberal thinkers have circulated accusations depicting conservative Christians as ignorant and foolish in their views on this subject. They have muddied the waters with accusations that, by and large, are "straw men," verbal tools to discredit what they do not accept or perhaps do not understand. This is the old game of ridiculing your opponent in a debate and intimidating him rather than honestly facing up to his arguments. At this point it is necessary to destroy some of these "straw men" that have been unjustly set up and frequently used. To do that, we need first of all to say what biblical inspiration *does not* mean.

Mechanical Dictation

It does not mean *mechanical dictation*—that is, that God dictated the material to the writers as a businessman would to his secretary. I do not know of any modern evangelical scholar who believes in mechanical dictation. Yet this "straw man" is constantly thrown up against conservative Christians. In spite of many denials, in spite of all of the evidence to the contrary, opponents are still using this old, moth-eaten argument. It needs to be asserted one more time that *we do not believe in mechanical dictation.* The definition of inspiration which reflects the classic understanding of the church is this: God so supernaturally directed the writers of Scripture that without waiving their human intelligence, literary style, or personal feeling, His complete and coherent message to man was recorded with perfect accuracy, the very words of the original Scripture bearing the authority of divine authorship. God used the human intelligence, the literary style, the personal feelings of each author. He did not override them. He did not force material through a reluctant penman. He supernaturally prepared the penman.

Some people in B. B. Warfield's day (the late nineteenth century) were saying that inspiration might be compared with sunlight shining through a stained-glass window into a cathedral. They claimed that just as the stained-glass colors the light and changes its hue, so God's truth, when it passes through imperfect man, is bound to emerge differently from what it was originally. Therefore, they said, we cannot eliminate this aspect of humanity in Scripture.

Warfield, in his customary logical fashion, took their illustration and turned it around. Of course, we could think of the truth of God as light coming from Him, passing through a stained-glass window into a cathedral. But he asked: Did it ever occur to you that the architect who designed the cathedral designed that stained glass in precisely such a manner as to give the exact hue to the light that the window does give? Therefore, rather than the light being discolored, it is colored precisely as the architect wished it to be colored, to give just the proper tone and balance to the interior lighting of the cathedral. Warfield then proceeded to apply this analogy. When God decided to bring Paul's epistles into being, for example:

> He was not reduced to the necessity of going
> down to earth and painfully scrutinizing the men
> He found there, seeking anxiously for the one who,
> on the whole, promised best for His purpose, then
> violently forcing the material He wished to express
> through him, against his natural bent and with
> as little loss from his recalcitrant characteristics
> as possible. Nothing of the sort took place. If
> God wished to give His people a series of letters
> like Paul's, He prepared a Paul to write them.
> The Paul he brought to the task was a Paul who
> spontaneously would write just such letters.[1]

This old "straw man" about mechanical dictation should be rejected once more and, hopefully, laid to rest.

Only the Originals Are Inspired

Second, biblical inspiration does not mean *that the translations or editions or versions are inspired.* Only the original manuscripts, the *autographa*, are. This has also caused a lot of furor today. There are those who are saying that this does not really make sense, that since we do not have the original manuscripts it makes no difference whether the originals were inspired or not. It is a cop-out, they say, to claim that scribal errors have been made, for example, when we do not have the originals to prove it.

Some critics also assert that the idea of inerrancy as applying only to the *autographa* is a very recent view and that it never occurred to the ancients. Listen to Warfield again:

> This is a rather serious arraignment of the common sense of the whole series of preceding generations. Are we to believe that no man until our wonderful nineteenth century ever had acumen enough to detect a printer's error or to realize the liability of hand-copied manuscripts to occasional corruption? Are we really to believe that the happy possessors of the so-called "wicked Bible" held "thou shalt commit adultery" to be as divinely inerrant as the genuine text of the seventh commandment, on the ground that the inerrancy of the original autographs of the Holy Scriptures must not be asserted as distinguished from the Holy Scriptures which we now possess? Of course, every man of common sense, from the beginning of the world, has recognized the difference between the genuine text and the errors of transmission and has attached his confidence to the former in rejection of the latter.[2]

Warfield goes on to say: "Everybody knows that no book was ever printed, much less hand-copied, into which some errors did not intrude in the process. As we do not hold the author responsible for these in an ordinary book, neither ought we to hold God responsible for them in this extraordinary book which we call the Bible."[3]

Consider this statement from Augustine: "I do not doubt that their authors [the biblical authors] therein made no mistake and set forth nothing that might mislead. If, in one of these books, I stumble across something that seems opposed to the truth, I have no hesitation in saying that either my copy is faulty or the translator has not fully grasped what was said, or else I myself have not fully understood."[4]

Notice that as far back as Augustine, there was clear understanding of the difference between the original manuscript and the copy or edition which he might have in his hand. If there was an error, it might be in the copy, but it would not be in the original.

Another question arises. Why would God allow the originals to perish if they are so important? We certainly do not know for sure, but Thomas Grantham, an early Baptist mentioned previously, had a noteworthy comment. Grantham said that perhaps God allowed the *autographa* to perish because, if they had survived, they might have fallen into unscrupulous hands and been altered so as to produce heresy; then there would be no way to restore the original readings. Whereas, under the present circumstances, nobody anywhere has the lock on all of the existing manuscripts of Scripture. Some of the earliest, most reliable manuscripts are in the Vatican Library, some are in the British Museum, others are in museums and universities scattered around the United States. But altogether, through the process of textual criticism, we have essentially restored the *autographa*.

Whether this is the reason why we do not possess the originals or not, this at least makes good sense and certainly answers the question as to why we make so much of the originals when, as a matter of fact, we do not have them.

The Human Element

Third, biblical inspiration *does not eliminate the human element in Scripture.* The human element is there, in vocabulary, in style, in the way people say things, the way they think. But the point is that God superintended the process so that no error intruded into the text. Some today are saying that unless we rule out the human aspect of Scripture altogether, we have to agree that the biblical writers were omniscient and sinless. This is so, they say, because if there were any flaw in their knowledge or character, they obviously would have written Scripture that was flawed and, in some ways, obviously wrong. But that is not necessarily true at all. The doctrine of inspiration simply says that God the Holy Spirit superintended, He overruled their particular imperfections, and did not allow these imperfections to intrude into the Scripture that they wrote.

For example, it is quite likely that the apostle Paul believed that the earth was flat and that if one sailed through the Pillars of Hercules he would fall off the side eventually. We do not know this, but it is quite likely that such was his belief. Some are shocked at this, but I think that it is probably true. The point is that it was not necessary for God to inform the apostle Paul concerning every aspect of human knowledge in order that he might write Scripture. Paul was never called upon to comment on the shape of the earth. Therefore, it does not make any difference what he believed about it. It is not necessary for the writers of Scripture to understand Einsteinian physics in order to be able to write accurate Scripture. What is important is that they not be allowed to introduce error into what they did write, and that is what we believe happened through divine inspiration.

Figures of Speech

Fourth, biblical inspiration *does not eliminate figures of speech*. This is where the word *literal* is somewhat unfortunate. When we talk about literal interpretation, some people take that to mean that we believe all the Bible is to be interpreted in a very plastic, literalistic fashion, ruling out all figures of speech. This is absurd, but it is a common misconception. There are twenty to thirty different kinds of figures of speech found in Scripture, and it is simply ludicrous to say that we do not recognize these. As a matter of fact, we need to emphasize that it is just as destructive of biblical truth to take a figurative passage literally as it is to take a literal passage figuratively or allegorically. Either will destroy the intended meaning of Scripture.

Let me give several illustrations of this point. The Roman Catholic doctrine of transubstantiation (that the elements in the Lord's Supper literally become the body of Christ and the blood of Christ) is a grossly literal misunderstanding of a simple metaphor. When Jesus declared, "This is my body . . . this is the new testament in my blood," He was using a metaphor which simply declares that the elements of the Lord's Supper represent His body and blood. By taking literally what was intended to be metaphorical, we find great misinterpretation and misuse of a simple truth revealed by our Lord.

Another illustration of this is found in Matthew 5:29–30. In these verses Jesus declares, "If your right eye causes you to sin, gouge it out and throw it away. For it is better that you lose one of your members than for your whole body to be thrown into hell. And if your right hand causes you to sin, cut it off and throw it away. For it is better that you lose one of your members than for your whole body to go into hell!" The cutting off of the hand and the plucking out of the eye are prime examples of hyperbole, that is, an intentional exaggeration given for effect. The literal understanding of these statements by some in church history has led to self-mutilation. Again, the teaching is in the form of hyperbole and is not to be taken literally of the destruction of these parts of the body. The obvious meaning is that no sacrifice is too great to avoid hell.

Perhaps it is better to say that evangelicals believe that the Scriptures are meant to be interpreted *normally* rather than saying that we hold that the Bible should be interpreted *literally*. By "normal interpretation" we mean that the normal rules of speech are supposed to be employed. Everyone intuitively uses these techniques every day. For example, if one says that a little boy is running down the sidewalk and that that same lad's nose also is running, most people use the normal rules of language to understand the difference between the two uses of the word *running*. The Bible should be afforded the same hermeneutical courtesy.

Approximations and Imprecise Speech

Fifth, inspiration *does not eliminate approximations and loose quotations*. We do this in common speech. Why should we not recognize that the biblical writers do the same? We frequently say that Jesus Christ was on this earth two thousand years ago. At other times, we say He was here nineteen hundred years ago. Both of these are acceptable approximations, and neither is to be regarded as an error, because they are not intended to be exact.

A biblical example is the account of Jesus feeding the five thousand, which is found in all four Gospels. No one really would be disturbed to find out that the exact number of the people present was 5,115 or 4,910. The number five thousand is an approximate, ballpark figure. It is an example of how an amount can be accurate without having to be precise. However, when in another passage John tells us that there were 153 fish caught in the net (John 21:11), we do not expect that there were 152 or 154 fish. In both instances, the common-sense rules of language apply.

We may say, for example, that the Bible teaches that God loved the world so much that He gave Jesus Christ His only Son to save us and if we believe on Him we will not perish. That is an acceptable approximation of John 3:16, but it is not a verbatim quotation. It is acceptable in our vernacular today. It was also acceptable in the day of the biblical writers, and it does not mislead or deceive the reader.

Exact Duplication Not Required

Sixth, inspiration *does not demand exact duplication in parallel passages*—such as in the Gospel accounts. Even when there is an apparent discrepancy, we should be cautious and patient. The assumed or presumed discrepancies may well result from our incomplete understanding. Kenneth Kantzer, former dean of Trinity Evangelical Divinity School and former editor of *Christianity Today,* gives an interesting illustration of this from his own experience. A friend of his was rushed to the hospital in critical condition. One person told Dr. Kantzer that his friend was on foot and had been struck by an automobile, injured, and taken to the hospital. Someone else called him shortly thereafter and said that his friend was riding in an automobile, that there had been an accident, and that his friend was injured and taken to the hospital.

Dr. Kantzer did not know which one to believe. On the face of it, the reports appeared to be contradictory. But he later found out that both reports were true. His friend had indeed been hit as a pedestrian and placed in an ambulance, but while en route to the hospital, the ambulance was involved in an accident and the friend had sustained further injuries in this second accident.

That may be a bit unusual, but it demonstrates the fact that two partial accounts may both be accurate, even though they seem to be contradictory. When all the information is in, they may both prove to be right. Since we do not know precisely what took place on the occasions when Jesus spoke and did certain things, we must be very cautious about presuming so-called "error" just because of differences in the accounts. It is more likely that when all the facts are known to us eventually, we will find that they are perfectly compatible and simply give different aspects of the event.

Grammatical Conformity

Seventh, inspiration *does not mean grammatical and syntactical conformity.* Today, because of our schooling, we tend to think that people who do not observe certain so-called "rules of grammar" are departing into unacceptable speech. But we must be reminded that grammar is not a set of rules that we must obey. Grammar simply describes how a society has spoken and written in a particular generation and thus communicated effectively. Ultimately, what we are trying to do in speech is to communicate thought. If the thought is communicated adequately and accurately, the individual idiosyncrasies of grammar and syntax are not to be considered as errors, but simply as peculiarities of the individual writer, even as we have today.

For example, executive newsletters rarely contain a complete sentence. Everything is presented in staccato style—short statements such as "Boom ahead," "Inflation down," and so forth. These newsletters speak in a language which businesspeople understand. They are designed this way to communicate as much information as possible in a limited amount of space. This is not necessarily incorrect, nor does it confuse or mislead. Similarly, the fact that Paul begins Ephesians 3 with a sentence that has no verb is a peculiarity of his style; it does not constitute an error.

The King James Only Position

Some of our fundamentalist brethren are disappointed with the position that is laid out in this book because they believe that we have not gone far enough in defending the doctrine of inerrancy. They think we have ignored the full ramifications of the doctrine of preservation. They agree with the argument made by the moderates that the inspiration of the original manuscripts is insufficient to guarantee the authority of any of the translations of the Bible that we presently have. It is contended that the doctrine of the inerrancy of Scripture implies that God must also have inspired the translation process.

Generally, proponents of this position hold up the King James Version of the Bible as the inerrantly preserved Word of God for the English-speaking world today. Sometimes they will go so far as to say that there is no longer any need to examine our English Bibles in the light of the Greek text, but rather that the Greek text should be corrected by the King James Version.

There are several problems with this position. First, it commits the error of claiming what the Bible does not. The Scriptures never promise that a particular translation will be the normative text. The "King James only" position simply is not what the Bible claims about itself. Second, the view that only one translation is the preserved Word of God was not held by any of the Church Fathers, the Reformers, or the early Baptists. For that matter, it was not the position of the apostles. Jesus and the apostles used translations of the Scriptures and seemed not to have a problem with considering them to be authoritative.

For example, when Jesus quoted from Psalm 22 while hanging on the cross, He recited from an Aramaic translation of the Hebrew text (Matt. 27:46). Often when quoting from the Old Testament, the apostles relied on the Greek Septuagint translation. The only time in church history where it was asserted that just one particular version of the Bible was inspired was when the Roman Catholic Church made a similar claim about the Latin Vulgate.

Finally, it should be pointed out that the "King James only" position seems to be the result of Anglo-centric thinking rather than any careful search of the facts. There is no reason to believe that God loves the English-speaking peoples more than He loves those who speak other languages. Sometimes the argument is made that God inspired the King James translators because English is the predominant language in the modern world.

However, the truth is that there are now more professing Christians in Asia than there are in North America. Today, in the twenty-first century, a Christian is as likely to eat his dinner with chopsticks as he is with a fork! God is not an Englishman, much less is He an American. In effect, the advocates of the "King James only" position are denying that the authoritative Scriptures are available for those who do not speak English.

If the doctrine of preservation does not imply that only one translation is the Word of God, then how are we to understand the verses that declare the Bible is impervious and will remain until the end of time? Belief in the perpetual durability of the Bible is well-founded upon Scripture. In numerous passages, such as Matthew 5:18, God promises to preserve His Word. This is an assurance that the Bible will never be exterminated by its enemies, not that only one translation will be the Word of God.

One of the most awe-inspiring facts of history is that, in spite of deliberate attempts throughout the centuries to ban or burn the Word of God, thousands of ancient copies have survived and today the Bible is the most published book of all time. Christians have traditionally understood the indestructibility of the Scriptures to be the evidence of God's preservation of His Word. In order to hold to the inerrancy and authority of Scripture, it is not necessary or biblically defensible to hold that the King James Version is the only translation that is inspired.

What Do We Mean by Inspiration?

Let us now look on the positive side. By inspiration we mean that the Bible is accurate in all that it says and that it will not deceive its readers theologically, historically, chronologically, geographically, or scientifically. In other words, it may contain approximations, it may use figures of speech, it may use the common language of the day, but whatever it says, the Bible says it accurately.

Of course, the Bible is *not* a textbook on science. Of course, it is *not* a textbook on history. It is important to note that it is *not even* a textbook on theology! But whatever it says about *any* of these is correct, and no one will ever be deceived or led into error by believing what the Bible says. That is the crucial point.

Finally, let us consider terminology. Sometimes we speak of *verbal inspiration.* We simply mean that, in the original autographs, every word is inspired of God. Sometimes we speak of *plenary* inspiration. Plenary means that all the words are inspired—every one of them! Ecclesiastes is just as inspired as Romans. The Song of Solomon is just as inspired as the Gospel of John. All of it is God-breathed. *Infallible* is literally defined in the dictionary as "that which cannot deceive or that which cannot lead astray or be deceived." *Inerrant* means "without error." It is important to understand that *all of these terms say essentially the same thing.* The terminology is flexible. The terminology can even be dispensed with. No one word is essential, and everyone is not required to use the same words. One might choose *true,* or *accurate,* or whatever word conveys the same idea.

There should be no problem with or objection to "truth without any mixture of error," as stated in our Baptist Faith and Message, except that some people have distorted that phrase to the point where it is virtually meaningless. Of course, they can do that with every other term also. They can take the term *inerrant* and say that it means inerrant *in purpose,* that God accomplishes what He wants to accomplish through the Bible inerrantly, even though there may be factual errors in Scripture.

Those who criticize conservative Christians for using all of this terminology should consider the reason why we have to keep coining new terms to describe our position. It is because others keep usurping the old terms and twisting them into something totally different from their original meaning. Many of us would have no objection to speaking simply of the inspiration of Scripture, except that the term has been used in such diverse ways for the last two centuries by those who no longer believe in the historical doctrine that we have had to come to a more definitive terminology.

Take the word *Christian,* for example. Why should that not be sufficient? I am a Christian. Why should I have to say that I am an evangelical Christian? Why should I have to say that I am a born-again Christian? Those terms are actually tautological. They should not have to be used. They are redundant. But we feel a necessity to use those terms because the term *Christian* has now been usurped by those who are not really Christians. Therefore, we try to sharpen our terms in order to make absolutely clear what we mean.

The same thing is true of inspiration. We keep adding terms such as *inerrant,* or *infallible,* or *verbal,* or *plenary* because the simple term *inspiration* has long since been taken over by those who do not really believe in historic inspiration at all. We keep coming up with new adjectives in an attempt to preserve the original definition. But the terms are relatively unimportant. It is most emphatically not a problem of semantics. It is the concept that is important. We need to understand that, whatever terminology we use, the issue before us today is *not interpretation;* it is *not transmission;* it is *accuracy.*

In other words, it is not a question of interpretation, but it is a question of what the Bible *is* rather than what the Bible *says.* It is *not literal versus figurative.* It is not *that which we have* versus *that which we do not have.* That is not the point. The point is whether or not we can trust the Bible. Is it trustworthy in all that it says, not just in areas of theology? Is it our ultimate authority in every area of knowledge?

Historically, the Christian church has said *yes*, it can be trusted. It is accurate. There are those today, however, who are saying that the Bible is *not* altogether trustworthy and accurate. It is trustworthy, they say, in matters of faith and conduct, in matters of theology and morals, but not necessarily in matters of science, history, chronology, or geography. That position leads to the problems we talked about in the first chapter of this book. If we say it is not trustworthy in some of these areas, we have shifted our base of authority, and there is no intrinsic reason why we should maintain that it is authoritative in theology either. Scripture does not teach that the Bible is authoritative in some areas and not in others. It teaches that it is authoritative in all that it says. That is what Jesus said. Therefore, there is no logic in assuming that it is authoritative only in some areas and not in others.

We must emphasize that, according to the clear inference of Scripture itself, of Jesus, and of the Church Fathers, the Bible is either reliable altogether or else it is not necessarily reliable at all and thus may be suspect at any point. Who is to say where it is reliable and where it is not? The modern answer is that the Holy Spirit will guide us, but that is nothing more or less than existential philosophy. That is nothing more than sheer mysticism. That cuts the very ground out from under the ultimate authority of Scripture, because, as we have already seen, mysticism (for our purposes) is a form of rationalism, and it now becomes a basis of authority above Scripture. It means that the human mind is the grid through which all data and all phenomena must pass. It leads to an entirely different form of Christianity from that known historically and biblically.

Thus we come back to the "tragic step" with which we began. What is the answer? Is there any hope of salvaging historic Christian orthodoxy without some theological absolutes?

CHAPTER 7

The Next Big Issue for Christians: The Sufficiency of Scripture

"If Southern Baptists were to abandon the great truth of the sufficiency of Scripture, just at the time when we have regained the doctrine of inerrancy, it would be an ironic, but terrible tragedy."

RECENTLY, AT AN ANTIQUE STORE, there was an old instruction manual for blacksmiths. It was an exhaustive work with detailed directions on how to do things that most people would have no idea that a blacksmith ever did. The book not only gave instructions on how to shoe horses, but it also taught how a blacksmith was to do many tasks that would be done by a modern machinist or a welder. At one time that ragged old book may have been the final word on "blacksmithing," but the average person of today would not find it very helpful or relevant.

Unfortunately, this is the opinion that many people have toward the Scriptures. They believe that the Bible was the best resource for its day when it came to instruction manuals for living. But they believe it is too bound to its time and culture to be the final word on the difficult issues of our era. The Bible is thought to be like a sweet old grandpa: quaint, filled with interesting stories, but hopelessly out of date.

In contrast, Baptists are people of the Book. We know that since the Bible is the inspired Word of God, then it is "up to the job" no matter what challenge our complex world presents. The ability of the Word of God to address every area of human existence is called the *sufficiency of the Scriptures*.

An inerrant Bible is an authoritative Bible. Just as the doctrine of the inerrancy of Scripture logically leads to belief in its authority, even so the doctrine of the authority of the Bible necessitates the confidence that the Scriptures are sufficient. Christians did not arrive at the doctrine of the sufficiency of the Bible simply by way of logical reasoning; we believe that the Bible is the road map for living because it is what the Bible claims about itself. Paul told Timothy, "All Scripture is inspired by God and is profitable for teaching, for rebuking, for correcting, for training in righteousness, so that the man of God may be complete, equipped for every good work" (2 Tim. 3:16–17).

Because the Bible is inspired, Paul said, we can be sure that it is sufficient to equip us thoroughly for "every good work." Its divine origin guarantees that, as a guidebook for every area of life, it is more than adequate.

When we say that the Scriptures are sufficient for all matters pertaining to faith and practice, we are not claiming that the Bible gives exhaustive or explicit teaching about all things. For example, the Bible does not give specific instructions on how to counsel the victims of child abuse or how to provide treatment for patients with Alzheimer's disease. What the Word of God does provide is a set of clear teachings, principles, and commands that provides the Christian with the framework and tools to deal with all the issues of life. The Bible may not directly address such questions as whether abortion is ever permissible or whether it is proper to clone humans, but it does present a plain ethical system by which such difficult concerns can be answered. As Billy Graham says, "The Bible has the answer!"

Unfortunately, even among those who affirm the authority of Scripture there has been a tendency to deny its sufficiency. Today, the sufficiency of the Bible is being disavowed in a number of subtle ways: the preaching of the Word of God is displaced as the primary purpose of the worship service; the teaching of the Scripture is replaced by contradictory psychological and social theories; the doctrines of the Word of God are redefined so as to lose their meaning; and the revelation of the Bible is supplemented with claims of private revelation. What is even more disconcerting is that these things are often happening in Baptist churches and, yes, even in conservative Baptist churches.

The doctrine of the sufficiency of the Scriptures is being undermined in our churches with three dangerous errors. The first danger is the error of adding to the Word of God. This subtle blunder is as old as the Roman Catholic Church, but it is also the latest craze among those who are searching for extrabiblical, private revelation. What is so misleading about this error is that its proponents acknowledge that the Bible is necessary for salvation and service, but they deny that it is sufficient.

The replacing of the Word of God is the second danger facing our churches today. When the clear teaching of the Bible is replaced with modern psychological theory, the purpose of the church is no longer salvation, but therapy.

The third danger may be the most treacherous of all, because it is the least obvious. The displacing of the Word of God occurs when the preaching and teaching of the

Bible are relegated to the periphery of the worship of the church. This misstep is harder to detect, because in order to commit this error it is not necessary to do anything to the Bible or to its teachings—just leave them out. All three dangers commit the common error of undermining and denying the sufficiency of the Bible—the doctrine that the Word of God is the competent guidebook for every area of the believer's life. If Southern Baptists were to abandon the great truth of the sufficiency of Scripture just at the time when we have regained the doctrine of inerrancy, it would be an ironic but terrible tragedy.

Adding to the Word: The Issue of Private Revelation

The historical roots of the issue of *sola Scriptura* (Scripture alone) are found in the controversies between Protestants and Catholics during the Reformation. At the Council of Trent in 1545, the Roman Catholic Church officially rejected the doctrine of the sufficiency of Scripture. The Roman Church affirms that the Bible is the inspired revelation of God, but it also contends that the Catholic Church is the only competent interpreter of the Bible. Traditional Catholicism argues that it is the only vehicle through which the blessings of the Bible are conveyed.

The rejection of the sufficiency of Scripture by the Catholic Church results in two serious errors. First, it leads to the position that active membership in the Roman Church is necessary for salvation. Traditional Catholicism argues that without the sacraments provided by the Catholic Church—baptism, the Mass, confession to a priest, etc.—simple faith in the finished work of Christ is not enough. In others words, without the Catholic Church the Scriptures are not sufficient and the simple message of the Good News falls short. This heresy has a long history.

As early as the fifth century, Augustine decreed: "Outside the Church [a person] can have everything except salvation. He can have honor, he can have sacraments, he can sing alleluia, he can respond with Amen, he can have the Gospel, he can hold and preach the faith in the name of the Father and the Son and the Holy Spirit: but nowhere else than in the Catholic Church can he find salvation."[1]

Note that Augustine did not just argue that the sacraments are necessary for salvation—but that only those administered by *the Catholic Church* will save.

The second error brought about by the Catholic's denial of the sufficiency of Scripture is the contention that the guidance of the Roman Catholic Church is necessary for a correct understanding of the Bible. They believe that the bishops and the pope are the only competent interpreters of the Scriptures. This is why for centuries the Catholic Church forbade access to the Scriptures for the population as a whole and persecuted anyone who would dare attempt to make the Bible freely available.

Even today, many Catholic writers argue that the Bible by itself is not capable of providing the instructions necessary for either salvation or Christian service. A recent example of this is a compendium published by a group of Catholic apologists entitled *Not by Scripture Alone*. The title says it all. The Catholic Church commits the error of adding to the Word of God by claiming that its interpretation is a necessary component in properly understanding the Bible.

By contrast, Luther, Calvin, and the Anabaptists strongly affirmed the doctrine of *sola Scriptura* as the historic teaching of the early church. By *sola Scriptura* the Reformers meant that the Bible is all that is necessary for faith and practice. The gospel alone is the power of

God unto salvation. Historically, Baptists have recognized the sufficiency of Scripture and soul competency as twin doctrines. Because the Bible is God's condescending revelation to us, and because believers have the indwelling Holy Spirit within them, Christians do not have to have a priest or a pope standing between themselves and God. Simply believing the gospel message found in the Bible saves us, and we are safely guided in daily living by obeying the Bible's instructions.

Logos Plus Rhema?

Oddly enough, the danger of adding to the Word of God in modern times does not come from the Catholic Church alone but also from within evangelical congregations. Today, many are claiming to receive special, private revelation giving them specific instructions supplementing the general teaching found in the Bible. Historically, this error was found only in Pentecostal and charismatic churches, but today it can also be heard coming from an alarming number of Southern Baptist pulpits.

Do Christians today receive direct private revelation? The answer of some Southern Baptists is yes. They contend that while the Bible is the revelation of God for the Christian church in general, there is a private revelation available for the individual believer. Proponents of this view affirm the inspiration of the Scriptures, but they desire "something more." Some insist that they receive private instructions from God at certain times—which they call "a message of knowledge," based on 1 Corinthians 12:8. Generally, they admit that these commands are not audible but rather that they are communicated through inner impressions or feelings. Yet they contend that these instructions are quite specific.

At other times these Christians will eagerly welcome the messages of certain televangelists and revivalists as "a word from the Lord" in spite of the fact that sometimes their extravagant and bizarre declarations do not square with the Scriptures and often detract from the Bible. This is a dangerous trend. To contend that a Christian must receive a private word from God in order to completely know and do God's will is to implicitly deny the sufficiency of Scripture.

Proponents justify their view that private revelation is available to Christians on the fact that the New Testament uses two different Greek words for the word "word"— *logos* and *rhema*. According to their position, the *logos* is the written Word of God, i.e. the Bible, intended for the Christian population as a whole, while the *rhema* is the personal revelation that the Holy Spirit gives to the individual believer.

Making this distinction between *logos* and *rhema* to defend their position has two problems. First, it cannot be justified by a careful study of how the Bible uses the two words. Any reputable Greek dictionary or lexicon will verify that in both the Bible and in extrabiblical literature, the words are used interchangeably. The correlation of *logos* and *rhema* is comparable to the relationship between the English words *stated* and *said*. They mean the same thing. Simply put, *logos* and *rhema* are synonyms.

The second and more serious problem with this position is that it has the effect of undermining the authority of the Bible. This problem is recognized even by some charismatics. One popular charismatic speaker recounts how, after preaching a series of Bible messages all week at a conference, a man came up to complain that there had been no message for him. "I'm disappointed. I really thought you would have 'a word' for me," he lamented. "I've had 'a word' for you all week," the speaker replied. If the Bible needs something to be added to it, then by implication it is not complete and sufficient.

It is worth noting that several major cults are based on the claim of additional revelation. Mormonism, Jehovah's Witnesses, and Christian Science—just to name a few— all base their aberrant doctrines on the claims of their respective founders to special revelation. Adherents of the private revelation position are sensitive to this problem. This is why they contend that the additional revelation of today is private and intended only for individual believers. In practice, however, private revelation has a tendency to become public. At certain conferences and on Christian television shows, the latest supposed revelations are excitedly reported. Adherents of the private-revelation position betray an attraction for the sensational.

The private revelation view is both unnecessary and harmful. In answering this error, it is important to keep two points in mind. First, the Bible claims that it has all the divine instructions that the church as a whole and believers as individuals need. David rejoices that the Word of God is able to convert us and then subsequently instruct us (Ps. 19:7–11). Peter says that as believers we already have all we need for "life and godliness" (2 Pet. 1:3). Paul declares that the Scriptures are all we need for instruction and correction. If we follow them we will be "complete" and thoroughly "equipped" (2 Tim. 3:16–17). The Christian who owns a Bible needs additional revelation about as much as the Sahara Desert needs sand.

Second, it is important to make the distinction between *private revelation* and *God's guidance*. We affirm that God is involved in the life of the individual Christian. When believers claim that God is guiding them, they are making a much more modest assertion than the one claiming to receive private revelation. God's guidance is the leading of God that occurs in the life of every believer in a number of providential and indirect ways. When someone claims to believe that God is *guiding* in a certain direction, there is the implicit and humble admission that he or she does not have an infallible understanding of the will of God. On the other hand, when someone claims to receive *private revelation,* he means a direct and unambiguous encounter with the Spirit of God and that therefore his knowledge in a matter is infallible.

When talking about discerning the will of God for a person about a particular matter, it is also helpful to distinguish between inspiration and illumination. Inspiration is the process by which God transmitted His revelation through human agents, namely the prophets and the apostles. The Holy Spirit's work of inspiration ended with the closing of the canon of holy writ. Illumination, on the other hand, is the present work of the Holy Spirit by which He enables the believer to discern the spiritual import of Scripture and how it is applicable to his or her present situation. Inspiration is inerrant and infallible; illumination is approximate and occurs in the minds and hearts of earnest, yet fallible believers.

This means that a good dose of humility is in order when one declares what he or she believes to be the will of God about certain situations. Often, a pastor will declare to his congregation, "God has told me that such and such is the course of action we must take," and they often make such claims without qualification. Generally, the pastor is not claiming to have received actual revelation but is simply emphasizing his confidence in a certain course of action as being the will of God for them. But it also sometimes appears that statements like "God has told me" are made for the purpose of cutting off any debate at the knees. Theoretically, if the pastor has received direct revelation to go in a certain direction, then any questioning is an act of rebellion.

Unfortunately, there have been times when preachers have made declarative statements about the will of God concerning the buying of property or starting a particular program, only to have the enterprise fail miserably. When this happens, many in his congregation are caused to stumble. This scenario is as unnecessary as it is wrong.

We believe that many congregations would find it refreshing if their pastor would honestly declare, "Brethren, I have sought the will of God about this or that issue facing our church. My desire is only to find His will and do it. After much prayerful searching of the Scriptures, this is what I believe God would have us to do. To the best of my ability, this is what I discern the will of God to be for us in this matter." Such modesty and candor surely would be appreciated.

A Lack of Caution

A number of conservative Southern Baptists must shoulder some of the blame for the inability of so many of our own people to understand the difference between guidance and private revelation. There has been a notable lack of caution on the part of a number of our best preachers in how they describe God's leading in their lives. At conferences and conventions, we have heard a number of nationally known preachers use such phrases as "the Lord told me" or "then the Lord revealed to me" during the course of their messages. Afterward, almost without fail, when asked to elaborate on their comments, they would qualify their statements by saying they were referring only to strong impressions made upon their minds or impulses felt in their hearts.

There are a number of reasons why ministers of the gospel must be careful in explaining how God is leading in their hearts and lives. First, to use language that hints at direct revelation is misleading. In the heat of preaching, the tendency to overstate something is understandable. But, the ability to speak with precision should be seen as a virtue.

Second, we must remember that our hearers are taking us seriously—maybe not as much as we would like—but they are listening very closely, nonetheless. We preachers want our congregations to heed the Word of God in a way that is literally life changing. They cannot be blamed for not being able to tell the difference between when we are speaking literally and when we are "speaking evangelistically." It is not helpful when we use phrases like "God told me" to describe our impressions. Thank God that His guidance is real in the believer's life! But to raise our inner impressions and interpretations of providential circumstances to the level of private revelation ultimately undermines the authority and sufficiency of Scripture.

Third, our hearers take our claims about how God is directly revealing Himself to us and apply them to their own situations in which life-changing decisions must be made. Some become discouraged when they do not seem to have the direct pipeline their pastor claims to have. Others are inadvertently led into the error of the charismatic movement. All too often, when our congregants hear a preacher claiming he is receiving direct revelation from God, the warning bells that ought to be going off are not. Why? Because even non-charismatic preachers have had the unfortunate habit of using similar terminology. We should reserve the words *revelation* and *revealed* and apply them only to the written Word and the living Word.

A fourth reason we should be careful in our terminology concerning God's guidance is that some have been led to flighty and unstable decision making by erroneous teaching. Following mere emotions and impressions have caused some to make unwise decisions and engage in bizarre behavior that cannot be justified by the Scripture.

A final crucial reason for clearly delineating between guidance and private revelation is that some Christians are making decisions according to "a word of knowledge" that is clearly contrary to the teachings of the Bible. The number of recent examples of those tragically affected by such private revelations seems endless. One dear friend's wife received a special word from God saying that it was permissible for her to leave her husband for another man— who was also married. Another acquaintance has rejected the doctrine of an eternal hell when he received "a word from the Lord" that annihilation is true destiny of the lost. The private-revelation view is a false doctrine that has had real consequences.

Recently a man who was converted and baptized in a solid Christian church revealed how it was that he eventually joined the Mormons. Saved as a teenager, he got away from the Lord after graduating from college. One day, despondent over the direction of his life, he prayed in his living room that God would show him what he needed to do in order to rededicate his life. As he was rising from his knees, the doorbell rang. It was two Mormon missionaries. The man interpreted this as a sign from God and subsequently joined the Mormon cult. How important it is to judge all our circumstances and impressions by the Word of God (1 John 4:1)!

Replacing the Word:
The Issue of Modern Counseling

The second error that threatens the doctrine of the sufficiency of Scripture is the danger of replacing the Word of God. This occurs whenever biblical truth is replaced or negated with modern psychological theory. One of the more controversial issues today is the proper role of psychology and counseling in ministry. There are many good and godly Christian counselors who are doing a wonderful work for the kingdom of God. Many pastors find it helpful to be able to refer those with certain problems to a competent Christian professional. Those same godly Christian counselors would be among the first to say that theirs is a troubled discipline. One Christian mental health care professional wrote in a peer review journal that Christian counseling by definition is supposed to be centered on Christ, based on the Bible, and led by the Spirit.

However, he lamented, the true state of affairs is that "some Christian counselors give only lip service to such a definition, and their counseling ends up being Christian in name only. They are Christian persons, but there is nothing that is uniquely Christian in their counseling procedures."[2]

The reason many find modern psychology so difficult to integrate with principles of the Bible is because of the origins of psychology as a discipline. In no small part, psychology developed in the late nineteenth and twentieth centuries as a reaction against the biblical understanding of man. Most of the founders of the various schools of thought in modern psychology—for example, Sigmund Freud, Eric Fromm, and B. F. Skinner—were openly hostile to any form of religion. Studies show that the overwhelming majority of practicing psychologists are "unusually irreligious."[3] In this respect, modern psychology is much like modern biblical criticism: Its benefits are real, but so are its dangers.

If the discipline of counseling is going to be a blessing to the kingdom, then there are three errors that its practitioners must avoid. The first error is the outright *denial of biblical truth*. This occurs whenever the clear teaching of the New Testament is deemed to be outdated. The following quote by a noted Christian counselor is an example of this error:

> I believe the Bible to be an internally coherent testimony of the believing community throughout a 2,000 to 3,000 year period regarding the mighty acts of God's redemption in the community's experience. I believe that testimony is normative and authoritative for us in matters of faith and life because it is a warrantable testimony and is God's universalized truth. This does not, however, force me to agree that the Bible is authoritative truth in matters which are not the focus and burden of that spirit-inspired, redemptive testimony of the historic believers. Moreover, because the Bible is a testimony incarnated in the human fabric of historical and cultural material, just as God's testimony in the Son of God himself was incarnated in that same human stuff, it is imperative that its human limitations and historical anomalies be differentiated from its redemptively revelational material. Jesus, for example . . . spoke quite erroneously in terms of a three storied universe, and imminent second coming, and the like. Humanness radically conditioned him with cultural-historical limitations as regards issues that were not central to the single truth of

God's testimony in him, that is, that God is for
us, not against us. Why are those who insist on
inerrancy as the only foundation for authority in
Scripture afraid to have a Bible that is at least as
culturally bound as was the incarnate Son of God
himself . . . ?[4]

The author of the preceding quote justifies his position
with the claim that the Bible is as error-prone and culture-
bound as Jesus Christ. We agree with him that the veracity
of the Bible is on the same level as that of the Savior; however, we believe that Jesus was inerrant and transcends culture! That author sees the Bible as suffering from the same
archaic shortcomings as the old blacksmith's manual. He
affirms the authority of Scripture in principle, but denies
its sufficiency in practice. With this logic, many modern
psychologists who identify themselves as Christian reject
what the Bible clearly teaches about issues such as abortion, divorce, and homosexuality.

The second error that finds its root in modern psychology is the *redefinition of biblical truth.* This is the practice
of using biblical terminology, but applying new meanings to the terms. When it comes to this error, Robert
Schuller, pastor of the Crystal Cathedral in Garden Grove,
California, is in a league all to himself.

His weekly television show, *The Hour of Power,* is
watched on hundreds of stations in more than 180 countries
with an audience of over 20 million people, making him
the most popular televangelist in the world. Replacing the
gospel with his pop-psychology of "possibility thinking,"
Dr. Schuller redefines nearly every major doctrine of the
Bible.

Consider what Schuller does with the doctrine of sin:
Every problem, every evil, and all sin, he declares, is the

result of people having low self-esteem. In his book *Self-Esteem: The New Reformation,* he writes, "I contend that this unfulfilled need for self-esteem underlies every act . . . over and over again that the core of man's sin is not his depravity but a 'lack of self-dignity.' Self-esteem is . . . the single greatest need facing the human race today."[5] Schuller's redefinition of regeneration is equally novel: "To be born again means that we must be changed from a negative to a positive self-image, from inferiority to self-esteem, from fear to love, from doubt to trust."[6]

The doctrine of the atonement receives a similar treatment from Schuller, in which he reinterprets the death of Christ through the lens of "possibility thinking." He states, "Jesus knew his worth, his success fed his self-esteem. . . . He suffered the cross to sanctify his self-esteem. And he bore the cross to sanctify your self-esteem. And the cross will sanctify the ego trip!"[7] Such a theology of the cross would be unrecognizable to the apostles.

Schuller is probably the most blatant practitioner of the error of redefining biblical truth and therefore is also the easiest to detect. However, this practice is occurring in more insinuating ways in our Southern Baptist pulpits. It is not helpful when preachers replace the biblical term *salvation* with the expression "getting connected with God."

Modern psychology is a source of a third type of error, which is the error of the *substitution of biblical truth.* An example of this danger is seen in the debate about homosexuality. In the scientific community, there has always been a dispute about whether homosexuality is the result of environment or heredity. In other words, are homosexuals born or are they made? Forty years ago the prevailing opinion among those in the psychological and behavioral sciences was that homosexual behavior in men was the result of being raised in an environment of a domineering mother where the father was either absent or passive. Often, it was said, many homosexuals were victims of sexual abuse by homosexual pedophiles.

In other words, a generation ago the prevailing scientific opinion was that homosexuals were made and not born. Environment was believed to be the predominant factor. This viewpoint was considered to be easily reconcilable with the Bible's condemnation of homosexual behavior, and as recently as the early 1970s, homosexuality was seen as a treatable and perhaps curable mental illness.

What difference a decade can make! The 1980s saw advances in DNA research, and almost every aberrant behavior was beginning to be seen as the result of genetic predisposition. Now, many assume that homosexuals are the products of genetic predestination.

Some psychologists and counselors who claim that they are operating from a Christian perspective argue that, in the light of the latest scientific research, the church should rethink its opposition to the homosexual lifestyle. But Christians must not allow the latest edict from the gay community, attempting to legitimatize their sinful lifestyle through the medical and psychological communities, to have veto power over the clear teaching of the Bible.

Christians must always maintain a watchful, if not outright skeptical, attitude toward the work done by the secular world. Powlison strikes the right note when he advises that we have a cautious wariness about the latest conclusions of behavioral scientists:

> Secular disciplines may serve us well as they
> describe people; they may challenge us by how
> they seek to explain, guide, and change people; but
> they seriously mislead us when we take them at
> face value because they are secular. They explain

people, define what people ought to be like, and try to solve people's problems without considering God and man's relationship to God. Secular disciplines have made a systematic commitment to being wrong.

This is not to deny that secular people are often brilliant observers of other human beings. They are often ingenious critics and theoreticians. But they also distort what they see and mislead by what they teach and do, because from God's point of view the wisdom of the world has fundamental folly written through it. They will not acknowledge that God has created human beings as God-related and God accountable creatures. The mind set of secularity is like a power saw with a set that deviates from the right angle. It may be a powerful saw, and it may cut a lot of wood, but every board comes out crooked.[8]

There is a place for psychology and counseling in the ministry. Even John MacArthur, one of the most severe critics of Christian psychology, is quick to acknowledge that it is "sensible for someone who is alcoholic, drug addicted, learning disabled, traumatized by rape, incest, or severe battering to seek some help in trying to cope with their trauma." He goes on to say: "Certain techniques of human psychology can serve to lessen trauma or dependency and modify behavior in Christian or non-Christians equally. There may also be certain types of emotional illnesses where root causes are organic and where medication might be needed to stabilize an otherwise dangerous person."[9]

Affirming the sufficiency of the Bible in counseling does not mean that there is no place for psychological theory or counseling techniques any more than the sufficiency of the Bible in preaching means that sermons are to consist only of quoted Scripture. What it does mean is that the Bible is sufficient to be the final authority in counseling matters. Any psychological teaching or technique that is contrary to the teaching of Scripture is wrong and dangerous.

Christian counseling must function on the premise that Scripture is the greatest psychology text that will ever be. Consequently, every psychological perspective must be held up to Scripture. If it matches, well and good. We should keep and use it. If it does not equate with scriptural realities, however, it must be discarded. That is the task of Christian counselors—to minister with integrity, living out what we say we believe as Christians and calling others to do the same.

The right and wrong use of psychology may be easier to discern than some on both sides of the debate are willing to acknowledge. If an examination of a person's childhood and background gives insight to some of the motivations for his or her behavior, then that is good and helpful. If those same insights are used to try to justify sinful behavior, or to reject the clear teaching of Scripture, then it is wrong. If behavior-modification techniques or certain medications are used to restore to a person the ability to control actions or emotions, then this is a wise course of action and can be justified by Scripture.

However, behavior modification or emotional stability must never be seen by a Christian counselor as an end in itself. The Bible teaches that people are truly whole only when he or she is in right and full relationship with God. Any counseling that does not endeavor to bring the patient into full submission to the will of God as revealed in His authoritative Word is truncated at best and ultimately may be harmful. The key to this lies in the responsibility of the counselor to both know the truths of Scripture and have the courage to use them as the center of the treatment process.

Displacing the Word: Modern Worship Techniques

The third threat to the doctrine of the sufficiency of Scriptures is the tendency to displace the preaching of the Bible in our worship services. The apostle Paul warned that a day will come when people will want to be entertained rather than taught the Word of God. He declares: "For the time will come when they will not tolerate sound doctrine, but according to their own desires, will accumulate teachers for themselves because they have an itch to hear something new. They will turn away from hearing the truth and will turn aside to myths" (2 Tim. 4:3–4).

Paul is delivering more than a warning; it is also a prohibition in which he forbids us from indulging in this error.

Many changes are happening in our worship services. Drama, choruses, PowerPoint presentations, and other innovative techniques are transforming the way worship is done in churches all across America. Some churches, however, are going far beyond the mere use of new techniques. Various churches, in the desire to make their ministry more seeker-sensitive and relevant, have relegated the preaching of the Bible to a minor role in the service. Some have gone so far as to remove from their sanctuaries the cross and other symbols traditionally associated with Christianity.

Innovation is not usually something to be feared. When confronted with something new, we all must beware of the tendency to chant the deadly eight-worded mantra: "We have never done it that way before." Without a doubt, many adjustments do need to be made in how we approach worship. Ozzie and Harriet and the Brady Bunch are gone. The post-Christian America of the twenty-first century that God has called us to evangelize is a nation of diverse ethnicity and disparate backgrounds. The danger in our worship services is not that major changes will be made. The peril that exists in times of change is that we will not keep the main thing as the main thing. And the main thing about a worship service is the *preaching of the Word of God.*

There is a big difference between being innovative and being pragmatic. Innovation in ministry is to be encouraged. Creativity is a gift from God and should be cultivated in our people. When believers use their gifts and talents for the glory of God—whether it is in a drama skit or a praise band—the work of the church is enhanced. The inventive methods of today can be disconcerting to those of us who were taught how to do worship in earlier decades, but they are very effective in communicating the gospel to a twenty-first-century world.

Dwight L. Moody is a good example of a groundbreaking innovator. Sometimes it is difficult for Christians today to realize just how innovative Moody was considered to be in his day. He realized that post–Civil War America was changing, and he adapted his methods accordingly, using techniques such as the citywide crusade and the Bible institute. A pioneer who was not afraid to try new methods, Moody always kept the preaching of the gospel at the forefront of all his ministries.

Innovation is not to be confused with pragmatism. Being concerned only with results and not with principles is to be rejected. Being innovative means that we are open to new methods of telling the gospel, while the pragmatic approach operates on the premise that the end justifies the means. Presenting the gospel in new and pioneering ways is in keeping with the New Testament model; concealing the gospel to keep from offending our hearers is not. Taking the pragmatic approach to doing ministry is human-centered and reveals a lack of confidence in the sufficiency of preaching the Word of God.

Two examples from the mission field illustrate the difference between being innovative and being pragmatic. The first example is the great nineteenth-century missionary to China, Hudson Taylor. Taylor created a scandal among his coworkers when he adopted the clothing and hairstyle of the Chinese. For some of the dear sisters at the mission, his shaved head with pigtail was just too much! However, Taylor's desire was to relate to the people God had called him to reach, and the Lord honored his efforts. This is a classic paradigm of one who is an innovator for the cause of Christ.

The second example illustrates the pragmatic approach. Matteo Ricci and Roberto de Nobili were sixteenth-century Roman Catholic Jesuits who also were missionaries to the Orient. In contrast to Hudson Taylor, they did not simply endeavor to interact with the Asians. Rather, they attempted to integrate non-Christian religions with Christianity. This process of blending Christian beliefs with paganism is called *syncretism*. The work of Ricci and de Nobili is a case of pragmatism at its worst.

The pragmatic error of syncretism must not be allowed in our churches. There is a difference between, on the one hand, examining our methods and cultural symbols in order to whittle away that which is unnecessary and, on the other hand, pragmatically modeling our services to appeal to popular taste. The latter approach of pragmatism does not see the church as a congregation of believers but rather as a crowd of customers. Employing inventive methods and styles in our worship services should be supported. But there is a difference between providing a platform for believers to take part in worship and relying on gimmicks.

The issue of the inerrancy of the Scriptures is being settled. The question facing us today is whether we have confidence in the Bible's ability. The errors of adding to the Word with private revelation, replacing the Word with modern psychology, and displacing the Word in our worship services all have a common trait: They undermine the doctrine of the sufficiency of the Scriptures.

During the sixteenth century, English privateers captured a fleet of Spanish ships that was making its way from the New World to Spain. Anxious for silver and gold, the pirates were furious that the vessels contained only sacks of a strange type of bean, which the pirates promptly cast overboard. The curious cargo was chocolate beans, which at that time was nearly worth its weight in gold. Eager for the quick riches of glittering plunder, the buccaneers foolishly threw away a fortune. If the church allows itself to be distracted from the wealth of the Bible, we will be discarding a much greater treasure.

CHAPTER 8

The Southern Baptist Convention and Authority: What to Do Now?

"Conservatives who have fought so hard for the cause of inerrancy, and have paid so dear a price, must not delude themselves into thinking that the issue of the authority of Scripture is the only challenge facing our convention. The authority of Scripture may have been the most serious and immediate problem, but it is not an unaccompanied one. In addition, success brings its own set of dangers, so a number of pitfalls are emerging to join the hazards already present."

WHAT SHOULD A DENOMINATION look like that is committed to the lordship of Christ and the authority of His Word? Since the first edition of this book, many changes have taken place in our convention. Conservative, Bible-oriented Southern Baptists awoke to what was happening. We realized that we are still basically a solid conservative people who are committed to the Bible as the totally reliable Word of God. We recognized that forces were at work among us that were contrary to our basic posture. On state and local levels the debate continues, but the Southern Baptist Convention as a whole has made a clear declaration about our allegiance to the authority of the Scriptures.

As conservative trustees were elected to the agencies of our convention, the termination of personnel from convention institutions was not demanded, nor did we endeavor to dictate a "creed" to which all Southern Baptists must subscribe. Although this has been the accusation, in fact it is not the case. What was accomplished was a definite course correction in which we returned to the historic Baptist position on the Word of God. And yet the question remains: since the convention has unambiguously reaffirmed the great truth of the inerrancy of the Scriptures, what should we do now?

The Progress That Has Been Made

Very soon after the controversy began within the convention there were calls for the establishment of the theological parameters to which a person must subscribe in order to be accepted as a professor at one of our schools, or as a worker, writer, or policy maker at one of our agencies (the first edition of this book was one of those voices). These parameters would operate as an irreducible theological minimum to which the convention would expect its leaders and workers to subscribe.

The purpose of these parameters was not to establish who could or could not be a Baptist, or even a Southern Baptist, for that matter. The autonomy of the local church is a bedrock belief that conservatives also cherish. But just as 1 Timothy 3 sets a higher benchmark for those in the offices of pastor and deacon than for those who are mere members of a local assembly, it is proper to set a standard for denominational leaders that is not necessarily required of every messenger of the convention.

The fashioning of this set of parameters was to be undertaken with two conflicting facts in mind. On the one hand, it is impossible to set up a rigorous creed to which all Baptists can agree. On the other hand, we cannot adhere to religious liberty to the point that a denominational leader can advocate whatever he wants and not be held accountable. Academic freedom cannot be scholastic antinomianism. We do not want to become so prickly that we make a litmus test out of issues like a particular view of the millennium, yet at the same time we cannot leave open the theological doors so wide that Mormons, Unitarians, and wiccan witches could be accepted as Southern Baptist missionaries and seminary professors. Conservatives were convinced that, somewhere between the extremes of creedalism and anarchy, there is the proper balance.

With this goal of the biblical equilibrium in mind, a number of steps were taken to determine our theological boundaries about the nature of the Bible. The first step was the formation of the Peace Committee. Established at the 1986 Southern Baptist Convention and made up of leading members of the conservative and moderate factions of the denomination, the committee demonstrated that the issues were theological rather than merely political. The Peace Committee met fourteen times and visited the six seminaries of the convention. In its report to the SBC, the committee observed that their meetings were dominated with the issue of the inerrancy of the Scripture, even to the point of preempting the committee's scheduled agenda.

The committee also reported the findings of its visits to the seminaries. It recounted that, even though the seminary professors by and large claimed a high view of Scripture, many held positions that were hard to reconcile with that claim. Many teachers denied the historicity of major Bible characters such as Adam and Eve, Jonah, and the prophet Daniel. The historical accuracy of the Bible was rejected, and many of the miracles recorded in the Bible were understood to be parables rather than actual historical events. The report demonstrated what conservatives had been arguing all along—theological differences, and not politics, were at the root of the controversy.

The next step that helped establish the theological parameters for Southern Baptists concerning the authority of Scriptures came about by a recommendation of the Peace Committee. It scheduled a series of national conferences, one on biblical inerrancy, another on biblical interpretation, and still another on biblical imperatives. Representatives from the conservative and moderate factions of the convention met and passionately defended their respective positions. None of the meetings struck a strong note of affirmation for the authority of the Scriptures, only a discussion of the concerns. They provided further confirmation to the finding of the Peace Committee that the theological differences between the conservatives and moderates were real and distinct.

The definitive step in reaffirming the proper theological framework about the nature and authority of the Bible came when the 2000 Southern Baptist Convention overwhelming passed the third edition of the Baptist Faith and Message. The language used by the 1963 statement that described the Bible as merely being "the *record* of God's revelation to man" was replaced with the declaration that the Bible "*is* God's revelation of Himself to man." The last sentence of the section on the Bible in the 1963 edition which reads, "The criterion by which the Bible is to be interpreted is Jesus Christ," was changed to say, "All Scripture is a testimony to Christ, who is Himself the us of divine revelation." These revisions were necessary alt the neoorthodox manipulation of the Baptist Faith and Message that was used to pit the teachings of Jesus against other portions of the Bible. The passage of the new Baptist Faith and Message signals the commitment of the Southern Baptist Convention to the historic position of the infallibility and inerrancy of Scripture.

Some say that the course correction in our denomination came at the expense of academic freedom in our seminaries. This is a serious accusation, but we really must question the sincerity of those who voice it. In the recent past when there were many instances at our seminaries where the conservative view was either ignored or ridiculed—all in the name of academic freedom—where were those then who are calling for fair play now?

Many seminary students cannot help but notice a curious phenomenon, one that has been confirmed by the experiences of many other student colleagues. Conservative professors generally presented all the various positions on an issue, while openly advocating what they believed to be the biblical view. By contrast, liberal professors often would act as if the conservative point of view did not exist. If academic freedom means that a professor is free to teach whatever he chooses with blatant disregard for the guidelines provided by the Southern Baptist Convention, then by that definition there is less academic freedom. If, however, it is understood to mean that all points of view should get a fair hearing, yet examined from the perspective of historic Christianity, then it can be argued that today there is more academic freedom. The students at our seminaries are still required to struggle with the difficult questions that challenge our faith, but they will find that the professors are fellow travelers of faith rather than hostile opponents.

The Pitfalls to Avoid

Conservatives who have fought so hard for the cause of inerrancy, and have paid so dear a price, must not delude themselves into thinking that the issue of the authority of Scripture is the *only* challenge facing our convention. The authority of Scripture may have been the most serious and immediate problem, but it is not an unaccompanied one. In addition, success brings its own set of dangers, so a number of pitfalls are emerging to join the hazards already present.

One of the first pitfalls is *the danger of Christian cannibalism.* Conservatives must not indulge in the tendency to internal strife. The apostle Paul warned about the dangers of infighting by describing it as a form of cannibalism. He states, "But if you bite and devour one another, watch out, or you will be consumed by one another" (Gal. 5:15). During the heyday of the debate, opponents of the conservative resurgence argued that the struggle over the Bible was a Pandora's box that would lead to endless bickering. They predicted that the conservatives eventually would turn on one another and perhaps would irreversibly damage the Southern Baptist Convention in the process. Some observers on the sideline are still waiting for this to happen.

For the sake of the cause of Christ, we must not prove them right. However, the evidence of history may be on the side of the prognostications of the moderates. It is an unarguable fact that conservative and fundamentalist movements in the past have had a track record of splintering and infighting.

During the Desert Storm war against Iraq, America and its allies suffered remarkably few casualties. But one thing that made the fatalities that did occur so tragic was that many of them were the result of what was called "friendly fire"—an expression that is an oxymoron if there ever was one. During the confusion of battle, one of the greatest dangers that a soldier faces is the risk of accidentally being fired upon by his own troops. Before we pull the trigger, we must be sure that it is not a colleague in our sights. It would be a shame if, after surviving the attacks of our adversaries, we conservatives inflicted damage upon ourselves in ways that our foes could not.

The best way for conservatives to ensure that fratricide does not occur in our ranks is for us to protect our hearts. For over two decades, inerrantists have been in a vigorous struggle with moderates over the future direction of the Southern Baptist Convention. A high-pitched battle provides an adrenaline rush that can be dangerously addictive. One can forget the real motives for fighting the battle in the first place.

It may be helpful to consider King David and his top general, Joab, and contrast their reasons for fighting. Together, they faced many battles side by side, risking life and limb, and won great victories. On the one hand, David was the shepherd-king with a heart for God who entered the fray because there was a cause (1 Sam. 17:29). Joab, on the other hand, fought because he was a warrior by nature and he liked to kill. Joab's impure motives eventually were revealed, and in due course he met an ignoble end. We must never fight the good fight with evil intentions. It is important that Bible-believing Southern Baptists are on guard spiritually, and we must always demonstrate the attitude of David rather than that of Joab.

Perhaps to be forewarned is to be forearmed. The entire conservative resurgence has been a precedent-setting endeavor, accomplishing something that has never been done in the history of denominations. Perhaps the Southern Baptist Convention will be able to break the mold in the tendency to spiritual cannibalism, too, avoiding the snare that has befallen other conservative movements in history.

A second pitfall to avoid is the *danger of Baptist exclusivism*. One challenge that has always faced Southern Baptists is how to maintain the balance between upholding Baptist distinctives while at the same time cooperating with the larger Christian community. As Albert Mohler, president of The Southern Baptist Theological Seminary, has pointed out, the guiding principle that Southern Baptists have historically followed is that "the only genuine basis of true Christian unity is a unity on the teachings of the Bible as commonly accepted and commonly understood."[1] No alliance can be allowed that would imperil our commitment to Baptist distinctives. Therefore, Southern Baptists have followed the policy of *cooperation* with other Christian groups, not *compromise* or *union*. This is why the convention declined the invitation to join the World Council of Churches in 1940 and later declined similar offers to join the National Council of Churches and the National Association of Evangelicals.

That being said, there is a place for Southern Baptists to be involved in appropriate interdenominational activities at various academic, theological, social, and spiritual levels. Many conservative Southern Baptist seminary professors are involved in nondenominational academic pursuits such as the Evangelical Theological Society. Southern Baptists have taken part in certain interdenominational organizations such as the International Council on Biblical Inerrancy and the Council for Biblical Manhood and Womanhood. It is appropriate for Southern Baptists to cooperate with like-minded non-Baptists concerning social and moral issues such as abortion and religious liberty. And Southern Baptists have been active participants in the interdenominational crusades of evangelists such as D. L. Moody, Billy Sunday, and Billy Graham. Baptist polity does not require that we be isolationists.

We must never succumb to a Baptist version of "Campbellism," where Southern Baptists operate from the position that we can have no involvement at any level with non-Southern Baptists. The watchword for the inter-denominational relationships for Southern Baptists is *cooperation without compromise.*

A third potential pitfall to avoid is the *danger of a passionless orthodoxy.* It is possible to be doctrinally correct while comfortably complacent. The last attitude that we need to adopt is a maintenance mentality that turns inward. We will not evangelize the world if we merely try to hold on to what we already have by circling the wagons rather than forging ahead to new territory. If we become satisfied with a dry-eyed orthodoxy, then we will condemn ourselves to a slow, demoralizing decline. As the next section will show, however, our future is much brighter.

The Potential of the Future

These are exciting days to be serving the Lord. If we were free to live at any time in history at the place of our choice, many of us would choose to live for God in the Southern Baptist Convention at the beginning of the twenty-first century. God has blessed us with opportunities for advancing the kingdom of God that are stunning. The potential exists for seeing goals achieved in our lifetime that our forefathers could only dream about. Whether we make the best of our opportunities depends on if we will retain our *dedication to missions,* overcome the *challenge of the plateau,* and make good on our *commitment to change.*

Dedication to missions must always be the point on the arrow for Southern Baptists. In the final analysis, it is the reason for our convention's existence. Submission to the authority of the Scriptures and a commitment to missions go hand in hand, because it is through the Bible that our Lord gives us His Great Commission to evangelize the world.

The first edition of this book reported about the precipitous drop of the number of missionaries sent overseas by the mainline denominations. During the twenty-year period from 1960 to 1980, the decline in the number of foreign missionaries was 79 percent in the Episcopal church, 70 percent in the Lutheran Church in America, 70 percent in the United Presbyterian Church, 68 percent in the United Church of Christ, 66 percent in the Christian Church, and 46 percent in the United Methodist Church. This demonstrates the fact that when biblical authority as a base of theology begins to wane, missions and evangelism also decline very quickly. When a person begins to doubt the authority of Scripture, or, to put it another way, when human reason is substituted for divine revelation, this inevitably cuts the very nerve of evangelism and missions.

How has the cause of missions fared in the Southern Baptist Convention under conservative leadership? Critics of the conservative resurgence predicted that the efforts to restore fidelity to the Bible would result in a decline in mission activity. The statistics for the decade of the 1990s indicate that the exact opposite is true. From 1990 to 1999, the rate of new missionaries being commissioned grew 118 percent to over nine hundred per year; the number of full-time mission personnel grew 33 percent to over five thousand; and the number of short-term mission volunteers grew 170 percent to nearly twenty-six thousand. During the same time period, the results on the mission field have been just as astounding. The rate of new church starts grew 135 percent to nearly five thousand per year; the number of mission points grew 87 percent to over thirty-eight thousand; and, incredibly, the rate of baptisms overseas grew 116 percent to over four hundred and fifty thousand per year. These figures are staggering, and for them we praise God.

The work of international missions may be progressing wonderfully, but at home the Southern Baptist Convention faces *the challenge of the plateau.* We mentioned earlier that our convention did something no other denomination had ever done before when it halted the slide toward liberalism and returned to its biblical moorings. Now the time has come for Southern Baptists once again to do something that so far no denomination has been able to pull off: grow again after having plateaued. Over 70 percent of Southern Baptist churches are experiencing either no growth or are in decline. Sound doctrine is a necessary condition for healthy churches, but it is not a sufficient one. There also must be a passion for God and a zeal to win the lost. There are reasons for optimism. The fact that over five thousand churches are participating in the FAITH Sunday School Evangelism Program, is just one sign that there is a renewed commitment among Southern Baptists to soul-winning.

The return of the Southern Baptist Convention to the authority of Scriptures should be the first step of a *commitment to change.* Our vision for the convention is that we would become an organization of true churches filled with true believers. If we are under the authority of the Scripture, we have to take the claims of Scripture seriously. That type of commitment speaks of integrity, diligence, compassion, and a passion for God and for His gospel. A convention under the authority of the Word will have a vision for the energetic and visionary taking of the gospel into the marketplace of our culture and for the development of a distinctive Christian worldview that impacts the way we think, act, and make our decisions.

The Southern Baptist Convention that we envision is a denomination populated with stable homes directed by godly parents who nurture growing and obedient children. This would mean that our churches would be filled with husbands and wives who give themselves for each other as Paul describes in Ephesians 5. In a day when the traditional family is experiencing a meltdown, a happy home is a powerful and effective witness of the transforming grace of God.

A convention of churches under the authority of God's Word would be free from the bondage of debt and dependence on worldly and material burdens. This in turn would mean that we would have sufficient funds to flood the world with the message of the gospel. The Scriptures provide us with God's stewardship plan of all we are—body, mind, possessions, and talents. A denomination under the lordship of Christ will gladly follow His guidelines about money.

What would the Southern Baptist Convention look like if it were completely under the lordship of Christ? We would be a people of the highest standards of morality and ethics. Slander and misrepresentation, which abound in the world, would be absent from our churches. Trust and genuine fellowship would exist because we bow before a common Lord with a commitment to His Word. Our people and our churches would be growing, and the gospel would be news again because of the faithfulness of God's people—not because of the notoriety of the failure of professing Christians.

The future Southern Baptist churches would be challenging the culture, maintaining the faith of our fathers and the traditions of the past with a willingness to change methods and techniques to get the message out, but never compromising that message. The church of the future will be a seven-days-a-week, twenty-four-hours-a-day facility where there are many options for service for believers. The day of telling folks they have to come only at eleven o'clock on Sunday morning is gone. The communication tools of the twenty-first century—the Internet, television, radio, etc.—have changed all that. Like the twenty-four-hour stores and clinics, the church of the future will move toward timeless and endless opportunity. If Southern Baptists will truly submit to the lordship of Christ and the authority of His Word, the potential is boundless! We love our Southern Baptist Convention. Our entire lives are wrapped up in Jesus Christ through this convention. We must do something to maintain the strength and aggressive ministry that has historically characterized this convention.

We cannot allow the cry of "diversity" to intimidate us. Proper balance, within stated parameters, must be demonstrated and nurtured if our historical stance as Southern Baptists is to be preserved. These pages may not hold the final answer, but they are an attempt to help the Convention we love through days of struggle into victory for our Lord Jesus Christ.

Endnotes

1. A Tragic Step That Can Lead to Spiritual Disaster
1. George C. Bedell, Leo Sandon, Jr., and Charles T. Wellborn, *Religion in America,* 2nd edition (New York: Macmillan, 1982), 246.

2. The Dramatic Shift Away from Biblical Authority
1. George E. Ladd, *The New Testament and Criticism* (Grand Rapids: Eerdmans, 1967), 40.

2. Ibid.

3. Ronnie Littlejohn, "There Is No Sola Scriptura," *Christian Century* (March 14, 1984): 280.

4. Madipoane Masenya, "Biblical Authority and the Authority of Women's Experiences: Whither Way?" *Scriptura* 70 (1999), 229.

5. Mary McClintock Fulkerson, "'Is There a (Non-sexist) Bible in This Church?' A Feminist Case for the Priority of Interpretive Communities," *Modern Theology* 14:2 (April 1998): 225.

6. Stanley Hauerwas, *Unleashing the Scripture: Freeing the Bible from Captivity to America* (Nashville: Abingdon, 1993).

7. Benjamin C. Fisher, "The Challenge of Secularism to Christian Higher Education," a pamphlet published by the Education Commission of the Southern Baptist Convention.

8. M. Westphal, "The Cheating of Cratylus," *Modernity and Its Discontents,* ed. J. L. Marsh, M. Westphal, and J. D. Caputo (New York: Fordham University, 1992), 168.

9. F. Nietzsche, "On Truth and Lie in an Extra-Moral Sense," *The New Nietzsche,* ed. D. B. Allison (New York: Dell, 1977), xvi.

10. Gene Edward Veith, Jr., *Postmodern Times: A Christian Guide to Contemporary Thought and Culture* (Wheaton: Crossway, 1994), 16–17.

11. Richard Dawkins, *The Blind Watchmaker* (New York: Norton & Company, 1987), 6.

4. Baptists' Historical Position on Biblical Authority

1. W. T. Whitley, ed., *The Works of John Smyth*, 2 vols. (London: Cambridge University Press, 1915), 1:279, quoted in L. Russ Bush and Tom J. Nettles, *Baptists and the Bible*, rev. ed. (Nashville: Broadman & Holman, 1999), 13–14.

2. W. L. Lumpkin, *Baptist Confessions of Faith* (Valley Forge, Pa.: Judson, 1959), 122, quoted in Bush and Nettles, *Baptists and the Bible*, 16.

3. Thomas Grantham, "Introduction," in Christianismus Primitivus (London: Printed for Francis Smith, 1678), 3, quoted in Bush and Nettles, *Baptists and the Bible*, 25.

4. Bush and Nettles, *Baptists and the Bible*, 43.

5. Roger Williams, *The Complete Writings of Roger Williams*, 7 vols. (New York: Russell & Russell, 1963), 5:140, quoted in Bush and Nettles, *Baptists and the Bible*, 59.

6. Bush and Nettles, *Baptists and the Bible*, 83–91.

7. Francis Wayland, *Notes on the Principles and Practices of Baptist Churches* (New York: Sheldon, Blakeman & Co., 1851), 285–86, quoted in Bush and Nettles, *Baptists and the Bible*, 144.

8. John L. Dagg, *The Evidences of Christianity* (Macon, Ga.: J. W. Burke & Co., 1869), 230, quoted in Bush and Nettles, *Baptists and the Bible*, 151–52.

9. James P. Boyce, *Abstract of Theology* (Philadelphia: American Baptist Publication Society, 1867), 48, quoted in Bush and Nettles, *Baptists and the Bible*, 187.

10. Basil Manly, Jr., *The Bible Doctrine of Inspiration* (New York: A. C. Armstrong & Son, 1988), 29–30, quoted in Bush and Nettles, *Baptists and the Bible*, 191–192.

11. John A. Broadus, *A Catechism for Bible Teaching* (Philadelphia: American Baptist Publication Society, 1892), quoted in Bush and Nettles, *Baptists and the Bible*, 207–208.

12. Charles Haddon Spurgeon, "The Human Side of Inspiration," *The Sword and the Trowel*, October 1889, 551, quoted in Bush and Nettles, *Baptists and the Bible*, 227.

13. Bush and Nettles, *Baptists and the Bible*, 63–64.

14. Ibid., 64.

15. Walter Harrelson, "Passing on the Biblical Tradition Intact: The Role of Historical Criticism," in *Beyond the Impasse? Scripture, Interpretation, and Theology in Baptist Life* (Nashville: Broadman, 1992), 40–41.

16. Jim Rawdon, Letter in *The Word and Way*, August 24, 2000.

17. Marv Knox, editorial in *The Texas Baptist Standard*, June 20, 2000.

18. Kirsopp Lake, *The Religion of Yesterday and Tomorrow* (Boston: Houghton Mifflin, 1926), 26.

6. Biblical Authority: What We Do and Don't Mean

1. B. B. Warfield, *The Inspiration and Authority of the Bible,* 2nd ed. (Phillipsburg, N.J.: Presbyterian and Reformed, 1948), 101.

2. "Inerrancy of the Original Autographs," in *Selected Shorter Writings of Benjamin B. Warfield,* vol. 2., ed. John Meeter. (Phillipsburg, N.J.: Presbyterian and Reformed, 1973), 585.

3. Ibid., 582.

4. George Duncan Barry, *The Inspiration and Authority of Holy Scripture* (New York: Macmillan, 1919), 140.

7. The Next Big Issue for Christians: The Sufficiency of Scripture

1. Augustine, *"Sermo Ad Caesariensis Ecclesiae Plebem 6,"* in *Corpus Scriptorum Ecclesiasticorum Latinorum: Scripta Contra Donatistas,* vol. 53 (Vindobonae: Hoelder-Pichler-Tempsky, 1910), 174–75.

2. Kirk E. Farnsworth, "The Devil Sends Errors in Pairs," *Journal of Psychology and Christianity* 15:2 (1996): 123.

3. Eric L. Johnson, "A Place for the Bible Within Psychological Science," *Journal of Psychology and Theology* 20 (Winter 1992): 346–47.

4. J. Harold Ellens, "Biblical Themes in Psychological Theory and Practice," *Journal of Psychology and Christianity* 6:2 (1980): 2.

5. Robert Schuller, *Self-Esteem: The New Reformation* (Waco: Word, 1982), 15.

6. Ibid., 68.

7. Robert Schuller, *Living Positively One Day at a Time* (Berkley: Berkley Publishing Group, 1986), 201.

8. David Powlison, "Frequently Asked Questions about Biblical Counseling," in *Introduction to Biblical Counseling,* eds., John MacArthur and Wayne Mack (Dallas: Word, 1994), 365–66.

9. John MacArthur, *Our Sufficiency in Christ* (Dallas: Word, 1991), 58.

8. The Southern Baptist Convention and Authority: What to Do Now?

1. Albert Mohler, "The Southern Baptist Convention and the Issue of Interdenominational Relationships," sm.html, accessed February 8, 2001.

James T. Draper, Jr.

Jimmy Draper has served as President and Chief Executive Officer of LifeWay Christian Resources of the Southern Baptist Convention since August 1991. He is a graduate of Baylor University and Southwestern Baptist Theological Seminary. Before coming to LifeWay, he pastored churches for thirty-five years, including First Southern Baptist Church of Del City, Oklahoma, and First Baptist Church of Euless, Texas. He was elected President of the Southern Baptist Pastors' Conference in 1979 and President of the Southern Baptist Convention in 1982 and 1983.

Kenneth Keathley

Ken Keathley is currently serving as Dean of Students and Assistant Professor of Theology and Philosophy at New Orleans Theological Seminary in New Orleans, Louisiana. He graduated from Southeastern Baptist Theological Seminary with a Master of Divinity and a Ph.D. in Theology. Since coming to Christ at the age of seventeen, Ken has served as youth pastor, interim pastor, or senior pastor of churches in Missouri, South Carolina and North Carolina. Ken, his wife Penny, and their two children reside in New Orleans.